KE
PUB WALKS

David and Hilary Staines

COUNTRYSIDE BOOKS
NEWBURY BERKSHIRE

COUNTRYSIDE BOOKS
3 Catherine Road
Newbury, Berkshire

To view our complete range of books,
please visit us at
www.countrysidebooks.co.uk

ISBN 978 1 84674 341 2

Photographs by David Staines

Designed by KT Designs, St Helens

Produced through The Letterworks Ltd., Reading
Typeset by KT Designs, St Helens
Printed by The Holywell Press, Oxford

CONTENTS

The north Kent coast at Reculver with the famous towers and next to them the King Ethelbert Inn featured in Walk 16.

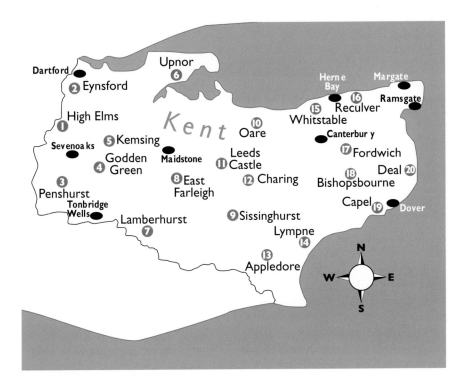

PUBLISHER'S NOTE

We hope that you obtain considerable enjoyment from this book; great care has been taken in its preparation. Although at the time of publication all routes followed public rights of way or permitted paths, diversion orders can be made and permissions withdrawn.

We cannot, of course, be held responsible for such diversion orders and any inaccuracies in the text which result from these or any other changes to the routes, nor any damage which might result from walkers trespassing on private property. We are anxious though that all the details covering the walks are kept up to date and would therefore welcome information from readers which would be relevant to future editions.

The simple sketch maps that accompany the walks in this book are based on notes made by the author whilst checking out the routes on the ground. They are designed to show you how to reach the start, to point out the main features of the overall circuit and they contain a progression of numbers that relate to the paragraphs of the text.

However, for the benefit of a proper map, we do recommend that you purchase the relevant Ordnance Survey sheet covering your walk. The Ordnance Survey maps are widely available, especially through booksellers and local newsagents.

INTRODUCTION

Kent and beer have gone hand in hand for centuries. Enduring images of the countryside include acres of hop gardens and oast houses where harvested hops were dried as part of the brewing process. It's not surprising that Kent has an outstanding selection of pubs for the enjoyment of the finished product. This book capitalises on that heritage, coupled with the outstanding variety of walks and scenery that the county provides.

We have chosen 20 walks, centred on a wide variety of pubs that take in the best that the 'Garden of England' has to offer. There are plenty of walks in the countryside, but we also take you along cliff tops, beaches, seafronts, through historic towns and villages, alongside wide open marshes and even to the end of the last seaside pier left in the county. There really is so much to see and do.

Each of the walks has been specially surveyed for this book. Even where we were familiar with the routes we have walked them again to ensure that all the information is as up to date as possible. Unfortunately, we cannot rule out the fact that changes to paths, gates, stiles and even the landscape are frequent. It is most unlikely, but if you are in any doubt about either the progress or safety of the route, or where a path has become unclear or obstructed, always be prepared to turn round and retrace your steps to the starting place. Don't risk getting seriously lost. Before setting out always allow enough time to retrace your route before the onset of darkness. A crisp winter's afternoon is a fantastic time of year to enjoy a walk, but don't forget how early it actually gets dark. Before you set out always make sure you take the relevant Ordnance Survey map, and that you know how to read it – we give details of the relevant sheet as part of the walk. The latest editions of the 1:25,000 series are by far the best. Where we suggest using a pub car park, it is wise to confirm at the bar that you will be eating or drinking in the pub before or after your walk. We found that every pub would accommodate dogs, although sometimes in limited areas away from dining tables. Unless we have included a specific note, each walk can be regarded as dog-friendly, with no major obstructions.

The beech avenue at High Elms Country Park

Walk 1
HIGH ELMS

Distance: 2 miles (5.6 km)

Map: OS Explorer 147 Sevenoaks & Tonbridge GR: TQ455633

How to get there: From the M25 junction 4 follow the signs for the A21 Bromley. The pub will be prominently on the left hand side next to the roundabout when you arrive in the village of Green Street Green.

Parking: Outside the Rose and Crown pub. **Postcode:** BR6 6BT.

The **High Elms Country Park** comprises 250 acres of woodland and open land on the borders of London forming the gateway to the Kentish countryside. It was part of the private estate of Lord Avebury, a scientist and social reformer – as a politician he introduced the Bank Holiday Act in Parliament. He was a friend of Charles Darwin who lived nearby, the two collaborating in scientific research. The land has been public open space since 1968.

This walk takes you through the woodland of North West Kent where you will come across many features left over from the years when it was a thriving country estate. You will walk down a magnificent avenue of beech trees planted in 1840 to the memory of a now forgotten baronet whist the estate features trees from around the world planted in the parkland. As you walk around you may also hear an iconic noise from another age. Only a few miles away, Biggin Hill airfield is now home to the largest number of operational World War II Spitfire Aircraft in the world. You often hear the noise of a Spitfire's Supermarine engine in the sky above you as you walk through the woods.

THE PUB — **THE ROSE AND CROWN** is a large pub in the village of Green Street Green. There has been a "Rose and Crown" alehouse at this site since 1787 when it was part of a collection of old houses and cottages picturesquely sited by a village green and pond. The building of the Farnborough Way by-pass road saw it all torn down in the 1920s to be replaced by a roundabout and the present pub was built in 1927 in a classic roadhouse style. It was extensively refurbished in 2016, providing a stylish modern interior in the leafy surrounding of the London / Kent border. There is an enormous garden at the rear. The daily changing menu varies around pub classics. Ales on tap on our last visit were Wells Bombardier, Youngs Special and Ordinary and Watneys Pale Ale.

⊕ www.the-roseandcrown.co.uk. ☎ 01689 869029.

The Walk

1 From outside the pub turn right into Cudham Lane North and then immediately right into Old Hill. Where the houses end take the footpath adjacent to the lane on the left hand side. Follow this up the hill next to the lane. It's hard to believe that this lane was once the main stagecoach route from London to Rye and Hastings. The old Rose and Crown was a stopping off point. At the top of the hill there

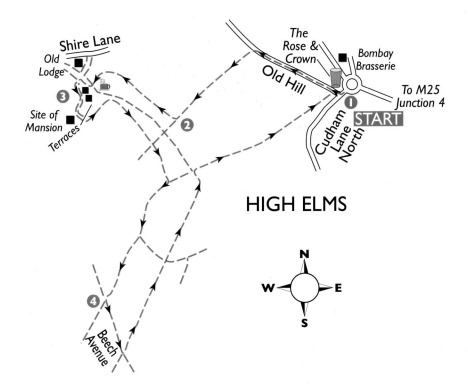

once stood a gibbet where the bodies of executed criminals would be hung in chains, swinging until they rotted as a lesson to other potential offenders – in particular highwaymen. Two hundred years ago, before the tree growth proliferated, the top of the hill would have been open ground and this deterrent on the main road would have been visible for miles around. When you reach the top of the hill take the path on the left deep into the woods.

2 At the next junction of paths turn right and follow the path all the way downhill until it curves at the bottom and comes out onto a drive, next to the old wall of the mansion's kitchen garden. We can recommend the café here. Turn right and then sharp left up another drive. On your left are the outbuildings of the lost mansion and the fives court. Follow the drive as it twists to the top and you come out at a flat grassed area, the site of the main house.

3 Bearing left take the steps up to the highest level of the terraces, turn left and take the path back deep into the wood. At the first main crossroads turn right. Follow this up the hill. At the top crossroads keep going ahead (signposted Beech Walk). At the steps at the end turn right (still signposted Beech Walk). Follow this path, where there is a divergence bear right and continue along until you reach the top of the Beech Avenue. Out on the golf course here one of the baronets built a ¼ mile long horse race course – it's said that 40,000 people were here to watch the last race in 1865.

4 Turn left and walk down the middle of the Beech Avenue. Notice new planting a little way down to replace trees lost in the Great Storm of October 1987. Half way down turn left where the path crosses. You now follow this path for as long as you can. At the end it curves uphill and at the crossroad of paths you immediately come to, turn right (signposted Green Street Green). Follow this path out of the woods and into the field. Looking out across the valley you can see the very point that the suburban sprawl of London ends and the countryside of Kent begins. Thanks to post war Green Belt legislation the encroachment of London was stopped in its tracks where it has remained ever since. Follow the path to the very end and it will bring you out at the bottom of Old Hill.

Place of Interest on the Walk

There are all sorts of reminders of the old **High Elms Estate** on the walk. The site of the grand mansion house, still surrounded by its garden terraces is now a grassy lawn at point 3. Built in the mid 1800s in an Italian style, it burnt down in 1967 but the corners of its rooms have been marked out in brick in the grass. Its surrounding gardens and terraces remain as a silent eerie reminder. Close by there are lodges, stables, a coach-house, kitchen garden, ice well, farm and even an early outdoor Eton Fives court which have outlived the grand house they were built to serve.

Clock House Farm on the High Elms estate

Lullingstone Castle

Walk 2
EYNSFORD

Distance: 3 miles (4.8 km)

Maps: OS Explorers 147 Sevenoaks & Tonbridge and 162 Greenwich & Gravesend – the walk straddles both maps GR: TQ 530630

How to get there: Eynsford is on the main A225 Swanley – Sevenoaks road. The ford is just off the main road in the village centre with the pub on the other side. We suggest you use the bridge as a popular local pastime is to watch overconfident drivers get stuck in the water.

Parking: At the Plough, but check the management is agreeable to your car remaining in the car park after you have left the pub. Postcode: DA4 0AE.

Eynsford's principle feature is the ford through the River Darenth, with its adjacent ancient bridge. There are also the remains of a 12th-century castle and a selection of ancient cottages scattered around the village. There is a keen sense of civic pride in Eynsford which has won many "best kept village" awards over the years – it even featured in its own documentary TV series. Right next to the ford and bridge stands the Plough, one of several village pubs.

The walk takes in a whole variety of features in the beautiful Darenth Valley. You will get some fantastic views as you gently climb the valley, there is a Roman villa to visit plus the chance to admire a Tudor castle gatehouse and visit the Lullingstone World Garden which also featured in its own TV documentary.

THE PUB As you can see in the picture, although lacking in a pub sign, THE PLOUGH has an enviable position right next to the picturesque ford and bridge. With crisp snow on the ground, a winter's day can also be a great day for a pub walk! In the not so distant past it served as a beefeater steakhouse but has now regained a new lease of life. Refurbished, the décor is modern with the bar and dining areas on different levels. There are some outside seats where you can take in the scene by the river. There are fixed price lunch menus and a la carte. Real ales on tap on our last visit were Greene King Morland Old Speckled Hen and Sharpe's Doom Bar.
⊕ www.theploughinneynsford.co.uk. ☎ 01322 862281.

The Walk

❶ Outside the Plough turn right. Follow the lane until it makes a turn to the left and there is a footpath on your right. Take this path up the hillside, cross the railway line and keep going. Where it crosses a lane, high on the hillside, take a few moments to look back down at the valley and village with the Victorian railway viaduct in the foreground. Cross the lane and follow the path along the top of the field until you reach the end at the tree line. Turn left and follow the path to the bottom of the hill.

❷ Where you emerge onto a lane, turn right. Follow the lane until you come to the spectacular Tudor gatehouse of Lullingstone Castle.

❸ Keep going a few yards in the same direction, then bear right past a barrier, and take the trackway on the right through the hedgerow. Follow the track up the hill but keep to the left of the next clump of trees. Now follow the broad grassy path up the hill. Where the paths diverge take the left-hand fork. Where the path enters a small bank of trees there is a post with red and black waymarkers. Follow the path

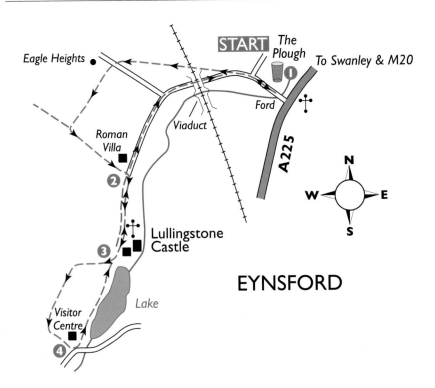

through the trees and you will emerge onto a field where you can see the Lullingstone Country Park visitor centre at the bottom of the hill. The country park was once Lullingstone Castle's private deer park. You can either follow the red waymarker straight down or turn right and climb to the top of the field. There are some benches at the top where we have sat and taken in some of the best views for miles around. Head back down to the visitor centre at the bottom of the hill. The café is a bit utilitarian inside but we've appreciated breaking a walk here for coffee on the outside benches.

➍ Now turn left along the riverside path behind the visitor centre. Follow the path back to point 3, then just keep following the lane all the way back to the start. Just after point 2 the large low building contains Lullingstone Roman villa. This is one of the best-preserved Roman villas in the country. It was established in around AD 85 and expanded until the 5th century when it was destroyed by fire. The site was lost until 1750 when workers installing fence posts for the deer park hit a

mosaic floor. Significantly the villa contained both pagan shrines and a Christian chapel and it was substantially excavated in the mid 20th century. It is open to the public. Keep going along the lane underneath the viaduct and this will bring you back to the Plough.

Place of Interest on the Walk

The present **Lullingstone Castle** building dates from 1497 although much of what survives is from the Queen Anne era. It has been home to the same family ever since. There was a silk farm here which produced silk for Queen Elizabeth II's coronation robes and wedding dress. The magnificent gatehouse dates from the 1490s and is thought to be one of the first ever to be built entirely of brick. Next door is the **World Garden of Plants**, created by the current heir to the estate.

Penshurst Place

Walk 3
PENSHURST

Distance: 3½ miles (5.6 km)

Maps: OS Explorer 147 Sevenoaks & Tonbridge GR: TQ515421

How to get there: Not that easy to find! From the A21 take the A26 turn south to Tonbridge. Take the next right (B2176) through Bidborough and keep going. This will eventually bring you to Penshurst village. Keep going through the village and out the other side. Turn right at the sign to Smarts Hill turning right at the top and then bearing immediately right.

Parking: Either the Bottle House Inn car park or the lane adjacent to the pub.

Postcode: TN11 8ET.

Penshurst is a small picturesque village in beautiful countryside. It lies between two rivers and is famous for Penshurst Place, ancestral home to the Sidney family and later owned by Henry VIII. The village is crammed full of medieval timber-framed houses and buildings of fascinating architectural interest. Cricket is still played here on one of England's oldest pitches, and the pubs don't disappoint either.

This walk starts from one of our favourite pubs with a ramble down some quiet country lanes before heading off across the fields. Once you are in Penshurst itself there's the opportunity to stop off for a mid-walk pint. Then you wander through this unspoilt village taking in the church and the stately pile of Penshurst Place itself. There is more road walking than some of our other itineraries but that's the best way to chance upon some of the architectural gems scattered around the village.

THE PUB | THE BOTTLE HOUSE INN was built in 1492 as a farm house, only becoming a pub in 1806. At one time parts of the pub were a shop. In 1938, extensive alterations were carried out, during which the two cottages into which the building had been divided were again made to form one house. The house was then licensed under the sign of 'The Bottle House' - the name coming from a large assortment of bottles that were found during rebuilding. There is an outside seating area to the front of the pub with a large dining area with all sorts of interesting nooks and crannies inside. Ales on our last visit included local brews Larkins Traditional, Tonbridge Copper Nob and Rustic. If visiting in winter seek out Larkins Porter if available! The menu is extensive with seasonal variations. The pub also promotes their own local walks with a couple of leaflets available.
⊕ www.thebottlehouseinnpenshurst.co.uk. ☎ 01892 870306.

The Walk

❶ Turn left out of the pub car park, carry on down the road following it left where another lane joins from the right and then go immediately left at the next turning signposted Penshurst & Tonbridge. Follow this lane to the bottom.

❷ At the crossroads (with the wooden bus shelter on the right) go straight ahead along the track. When you get to some cottages in front of you, follow the waymarker right. Take this path down through the trees and then out across the field. When you get to the tree line keep the trees on your left for a few yards then take the path on the left and cross the bridge. At the other end of the bridge take the left-hand path and follow it around the edge of the field until you come to a tree line at the end. At a T-junction of paths, turn left and follow the path to the very end.

3 At the lane turn left and follow the lane across the bridge into the village.

4 With the entrance to Penshurst Place on the right the road turns sharply left. A few yards later turn right up the steps through the gap in the medieval buildings – this is actually named Leicester Square! Carry on round the left-hand side of the church. There was a church

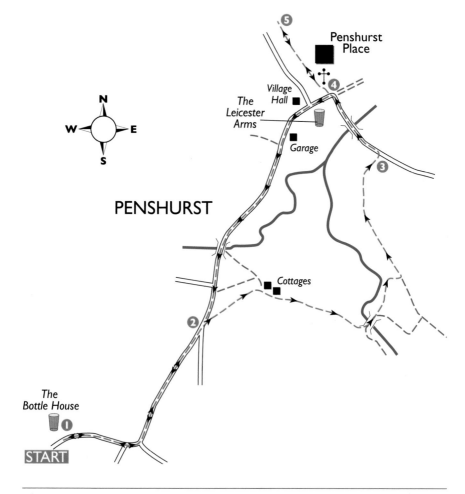

on this site before the Norman Conquest. In the churchyard in front of the porch is a rare survivor – a large stone table which was used once a year to distribute money to the needy of the village. The Grade I listed building is dedicated to St John the Baptist. Leave the churchyard through the gate and keep ahead along the path. Carry on up this path for as long as you like as it gently starts to climb uphill.

5 Behind you now is the chance to take in some views of Penshurst Place. Then return down the path back to point 4 (or alternatively walk back down the lane on your left as you are looking uphill). Once you have passed back through the medieval buildings, turn right at the bottom of the steps, the Leicester Arms is on the opposite side of the road. The Leicester Arms has a variety of cosy drinking areas with a larger open plan dining room to the rear. The menu features many pub favourites made with locally sourced produce. On our last visit Harvey's Best and Larkins Traditional were on hand pump.

⊕ theleicesterarmshotel.com. ☎ 01892 871617. You now carry on along the road in the same direction, all the way back to point 2, and then retrace your steps back to the start. Along the road take a look at the design of some of the village buildings; however diverse they are, many of them share a common architectural theme. The petrol garage really caught our eye. As well as the frontage, note the mock-Tudor side elevation. Although Tudor in style, many were built in the Victorian era. The large stone-built, timber-fronted village hall was built as recently as 1900.

Place of Interest on the Walk

Penshurst Place, once the property of King Henry VIII, was left to his son King Edward VI and granted to Sir William Sidney in 1552, whose descendants have been in continuous occupation for nearly 500 years since. One of the most impressive parts of the building is the Baron's Hall built in 1341. Surrounding the house is one of the oldest gardens in private ownership, a rare example of Elizabethan garden design. The family later became the Earls of Leicester, hence the village pub name whilst Leicester Square in London takes its name from the family who once owned another magnificent house on that site.

The medieval buildings at point 4 on the walk

Knole House

Walk 4

GODDEN GREEN

Distance: 4½ miles (7.2 km)

Map: OS Explorer 147 Sevenoaks & Tonbridge GR: TQ552551

Dog notes: Not suitable for dogs in the deer park.

How to get there: From the main A25 Sevenoaks – Borough Green road take the right turn in the middle of Seal village, then take the right hand fork. The pub is about a mile further on, on the right hand side of the road.

Parking: Outside the Buck's Head pub. Postcode: TN15 0JJ.

Godden Green is a tiny hamlet just to the east of Sevenoaks with a small cluster of houses around a village pond and green. Its position close to historic Knole House and Park ensures its popularity with visitors. Historically many of its residents were employees of the Knole estate. The Bucks Head prominently overlooks the green.

This walk takes you through lanes and woodland before emerging into Knole Park. In a rough figure of eight you will explore many parts of the 1,000-acre deer park and pass three sides of the spectacular Knole House. Featuring large undulating open spaces, together with dense woodland, the park has generally been kept in a traditional condition although there is a golf course in the grounds as well.

THE PUB THE BUCKS HEAD is a very popular Shepherd Neame tied house with a traditional atmosphere. The dining area is large but sympathetically split into different open plan parts. There are comfy sofas and in winter log fires. There is an outside drinking area at the front overlooking the green and a newly opened garden at the rear. The menu is extensive. Ales on tap on our last visit were Shepherd Neame Whitstable Bay, Master Brew and Spitfire Gold. The pub is closed Mondays except bank holidays. ⊕ www.thebucksheadsevenoaks.co.uk. ☎ 01732 761330.

The Walk

1 From outside the pub turn left, and then left again at the footpath sign by the post box. Carry on along this lane past the stables. When you emerge onto another lane turn left.

2 Follow this until the next footpath sign on the right which directs you down another lane. Follow the lane through the woods to the

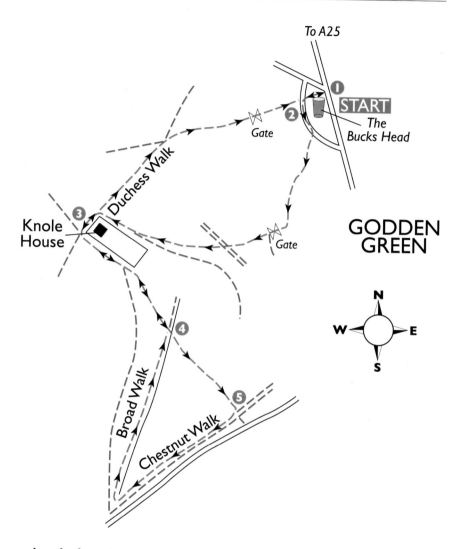

end and where it peters out, then take the continuing path that curves to the right. Go up the hill through the gate into the deer park. After you have passed through the gate take the right-hand path and then keep to the footpath to the right of the small pond which will appear unexpectedly in front of you. Keep following the path as it drops into a shallow valley and climbs up the other side over the golf course. Follow the path as it crosses a tarmac path until you reach the outer walls of Knole House. Bear right keeping the wall on your left as the path drops and then climbs again. After you have passed the restored barn on your left, turn left around the corner and you will be at the main façade of Knole House.

❸ Keep walking ahead with the frontage on your left and then turn left following the path round the far corner of the walled garden. Keep to the path with the walled garden on your left – you will have glimpses into the grounds of the house. After you have left the walled garden behind you, follow the path into the woods.

❹ After a few yards you will emerge onto the Broad Walk. Turn right onto the walk but then take the immediate left-hand turn off the Broad Walk and follow this path for approximately half a mile until you reach Chestnut Walk (another formal wide path cut through the woods) which crosses in front of you.

❺ Turn right onto the Chestnut Walk and follow it for approximately half a mile. Then take a sharp dog leg right, back down the length of the Broad Walk until you return to point 4. Now retrace your steps to point 3. At the front of the house, with the façade on your right, keep going straight ahead down the tree-lined Duchess Walk which starts opposite the restored barn. Follow the walk as it drops gently downhill and follow it round to the right where it emerges from the trees back onto the golf course. Keep following the path as it climbs the hill and after a while pass through the gate exiting the deer park. Follow the path as it passes through the woods, taking the right-hand fork near the end, and on to point 2, from where you retrace your steps to the start.

Place of Interest on the Walk⸻

Knole is ranked as one of the top five large historic houses in England. The National Trust thinks it might have been built as a "calendar house" having 365 rooms, 52 staircases, 12 entrances and seven courtyards. The oldest parts of the house were built by between 1456 and 1486. In 1538 the house was taken by Henry VIII, passing via Elizabeth I to the Sackville family who have been resident ever since. Urban myth has it that Hitler eyed it up as a suitable residence should his invasion of Great Britain ever have been successful.

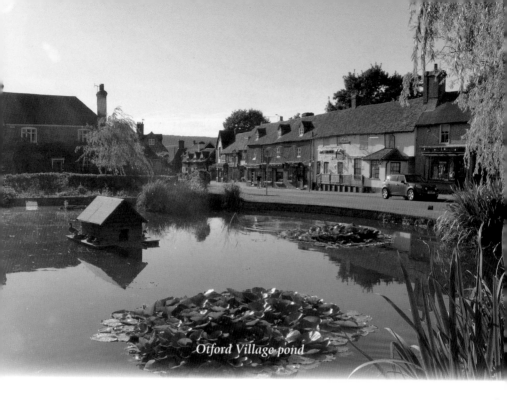

Otford Village pond

Walk 5
KEMSING

Distance: 4 miles (6.4 km)

Map: OS Explorer 147 Sevenoaks & Tonbridge **GR:** TQ 545591.

How to get there: From the A225 Swanley – Sevenoaks road take the signposted turn to Kemsing just to the east of Otford Station along the Pilgrims Way. Turn right where the lane narrows and first left which will bring you up to the pub about half a mile later.

Parking: Public car park almost opposite the Bell pub. **Postcode:** TN15 6NB.

Kemsing is a small village that nestles at the foot of the North Downs. Its most famous citizen was Saint Edith of Wilton who was born here in 961, the illegitimate daughter of Saxon King Edgar I. In the middle of the village there is a well dedicated to her memory (allegedly the water has healing powers) together with a war memorial, a cluster of ancient cottages and the Bell Inn which is one of two inns that once served the village centre.

This walk will take you from the village centre up the side of the North Downs through woods and fields with some stunning views. Half way along the walk is the chance to stop for a drink at another pub which has a truly unique atmosphere and charm. You then drop steeply downhill past Kemsing Downs back into the village.

THE PUB THE BELL is a typical village pub right in the centre of the community. It used to face the Wheatsheaf; the village's other pub across the road until that establishment met an untimely fiery end 2011. There is a cosy small front drinking bar which opens up onto a larger dining area. There is outside seating where you can watch village life pass by and a garden at the rear. A "Country Kitchen" menu is offered together with a large range of daily specials on a blackboard as well as sandwiches. Real ales on offer are from the Greene King range, on our last visit they were Greene King IPA and Greene King Morland Crafty Hen.

☎ 01732 761550.

The Walk

❶ Turn right out of the pub, cross the road and take the immediate left turn into the car park. Head in the direction of the church taking the path at the very end of the high brick wall. Follow it through to the churchyard. Despite the village's association with St Edith, Kemsing church is dedicated to St Mary. It is ancient, of Saxon origin, and sits slightly back from the centre of the village. Close by is the Kemsing Heritage Centre which is open on Monday afternoons (not bank holidays) and in the morning on the first Saturday of each month. Leave the churchyard by the opposite exit. Walk through the entrance to the recreation ground. A large clump of trees will be facing you. Bear around the left-hand side of the trees and you will see a hole in the treeline ahead of you where the path leaves the recreation ground. Take this path and turn right when you reach the lane.

❷ After about 300 yards take the footpath on the left. There is only a small sign and it is quite hidden. If you are still walking along the lane with open fields on your right-hand side you have missed the turn. Follow the path as it squeezes to the right of the high brick wall.

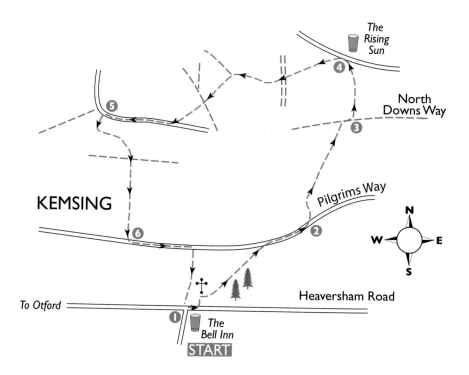

You now follow this path as it twists and turns through the woods and later across the fields. Take a few moments to look back at the spectacular views across the valley. The prominent church tower to the right is Seal church near Sevenoaks. Keep following the path uphill until you go through a gate and emerge onto another path which will be in front of you. This is the North Downs Way.

3 Turn right along this path for a few yards. At the next gate turn sharp left and take the path with the tree line on your left. Go through the next gate and keep following the path until you come to a road. The last few yards will be a bit of a squeeze! At the road turn left. Almost immediately on your right is the Rising Sun pub. The Rising Sun is like no other pub – it is utterly caught in a time warp. The outside will not prepare you for the inside! Don't expect any food but do expect to be able to talk to the dog, the cat, the parrot and the chickens. Take a pew on a sofa; it's just like being in someone's front room, because … it more or less is! Do stop by for a pint, you

will be richer for the experience. Over the years Clanconnel Irish Black, Holdens Stout and Westerham Audit Ale have been memorable brews.

4 A few yards after the pub take the footpath on the left – again it's a bit narrow. Keep following the path, after a while it will cross a track with metal gates and continue on into the woods. When you emerge from the woods bear left across the next field. Half way across there is a waymarker on a tall post. Keep going in the same direction. At the far diagonal end of the field go through the metal gate and turn right along the lane.

5 Where the lane turns to the right, take the footpath on the left. Now just keep following this path as it twists and turns. Where it starts to descend just keep going downhill. You will finally come out on Kemsing Down and at the very bottom there is a gate out onto a lane.

6 Turn left onto the lane and about 300 yards later take the signposted footpath on the right. This will bring you back down to the village centre and the start point.

Place of Interest Nearby

The village of **Otford** is a couple of miles away and has a whole host of historic features. Central to the village is the Grade II listed duck pond with its floating duck house. There are the remains of an Archbishops Palace built in 1514 which has included Henry VIII as one of its visitors, an historic church, antique shops and a model of the solar system billed as the largest in the world – to a scale of 1:4,595,700,000 (i.e. 1mm = 4,595.7km). If you don't fancy a pub meal the tea shop overlooking the pond (the appropriately named **Pond View Café**) can be recommended.

Oast house cowl

Upnor Castle

Walk 6
UPNOR

Distance: 4 miles (6.4 km)

Map: OS Explorer 163 Gravesend and Rochester **GR:** TQ757705

How to get there: From the M2 Junction 1 take the exit for the A289 in the direction of Grain. Then follow the signs for Upnor which will eventually take you into the village. Then follow the signs for the castle. Park in the free car park, there is little other parking in the village.

Parking: In the village car park. **Postcode:** ME2 4XG

Upnor sits on the banks of the tidal River Medway opposite Chatham. Its history is inexorably linked with the massive Royal Dockyard on the other side of the water yet it has remained a quiet unspoilt gem with a tiny cobbled high street flanked by listed buildings dropping down towards the river, and a 16th-century castle.

This walk takes you from the village along the shoreline of the Medway and then back inland through open countryside and woodland. Please note one vital point. The outward walk should only be attempted at low or near low tide. An easy way to check tide tables is via a link on the BBC weather website, then refer to either Upnor or Chatham Lock Approaches. You will need to wear footwear suitable for muddy conditions.

THE PUB THE KINGS ARMS has won the title of CAMRA "Medway Pub of the Year" for several years on the trot. It's situated at the top of the short High Street. It prides itself on being a family owned pub with a promise to provide excellent food at an affordable price. There is a separate bar and dining areas and a large garden at the rear. It's a freehouse; ales on tap on our last visit were Dark Star Hophead, Adnams Broadside and Mighty Oak Copper Tail. ⊕ www.kingsarmsupnor.co.uk. ☎ 01634 717490.

The Walk

1 From the car park follow the signs to the castle and High Street. You will quickly emerge onto a road opposite the Kings Arms. Turn left, and bear right at the junction keeping the high wall to your right. Follow the path with the wall on the right until you drop down some steps, then turn right along the road. After you pass the Ship Inn on the left, follow the path behind the sea wall.

2 At the commemorative obelisk keep straight ahead until you reach the entrance to the Medway Yacht Club, then take the path along the sea wall through the gate. Drop down onto the shore and keep walking along the beach. There is plenty of interest here. If you turn around there are fine views back towards Upnor Castle. You will pass two fortifications of different eras which are gently eroding into the waters. The crazy angle of the World War II pillbox is remarkable where land beneath it has been washed away yet its own stronger structure remains intact. Further on are the brick remains of Cockham Wood Fort. Built in 1669 it took on the role of defending Chatham Dockyard from seaborne attack, a role which had been performed by Upnor Castle for the previous hundred years. The fort was abandoned around 1818 after several decades of gradual dilapidation. You will pass the brickwork of the lower battery which is a prominent feature on the shoreline. After you have passed the fort the path climbs up to the shoreline. Follow it ahead with the boatyards and houseboats on the right. Follow the public footpath through the gate and through Hoo Ness Yacht Club.

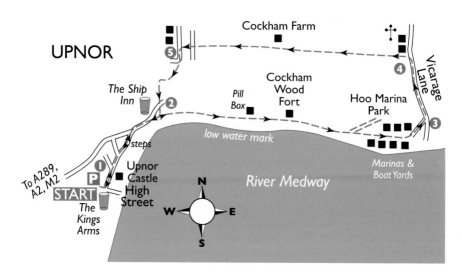

You will soon have a holiday park on your left-hand side. Keep going following the footpath signs with the boatyards behind the fences to your right and the holiday park on your left.

3 When you reach the security entrance to Port Werburgh turn up the access road with the port entrance now behind you. The holiday park will now be on your left as you walk up the road. If you are still walking with the shore-side boatyards on your right and the holiday park is no longer on your left then you have missed the turn. The access road emerges onto Vicarage Lane with a bus stop on the left. Keep ahead up the road.

4 When you reach the first of the houses turn left onto a long drive and just keep going. Keep ahead in the same direction passing Cockham Farm. Where the track finally enters a wooded area with a high wall on the left, keep going ahead. It will finally cross an access road to a new housing estate, and then it will narrow before emerging onto a residential road.

5 Turn left and at the end of the road keep ahead along the drive and then along the footpath as it drops into the woods. Keep following the path as it twists and turns down through the woods and you will return to point 2. Turn right and retrace your steps to the start.

Place of Interest on the Walk

In the 16th century, Queen Elizabeth I founded the dockyard at Chatham and it was decided to build a fort a short way downstream in order to protect the anchorage. Construction of **Upnor Castle** began in 1559 and lasted until 1564. Despite a brave attempt, it entirely failed in its role in 1667, when the Dutch sailed past it to burn and capture part of the English fleet at anchor. The raid exposed the weaknesses of the Medway defences and led to the castle losing its role as an artillery fortification. Upnor Castle became a naval ammunition depot, storing – at a safe distance across the water from the dockyard – great quantities of gunpowder, ammunition, and cannon to replenish the warships that came to Chatham for repair and resupply. It remained in military use until as late as 1945 and is now owned by Historic England and is open to the public. The entrance is at the end of the High Street.

Lamberhurst vineyard

Walk 7
LAMBERHURST

Distance: 2 ½ miles (4 km)

Map: OS Explorer 136 High Weald **GR:** TQ655358

How to get there: From the A21 take the right hand turn signposted road to Hook Green, a mile after the end of the dual carriageway Pembury by-pass. At the crossroads at Hook Green turn left and the pub is on the right hand side of the road.

Parking: At the Elephant's Head pub. **Postcode:** TN3 8LJ.

Lamberhurst is an historic village, it is said a yew tree in the churchyard is over 1500 years old. Until recently the main A21 ran through its centre but now the constant choking stream of traffic has been diverted onto a bypass leaving the village centre in tranquil peace. In the evenings it's an eerie contrast for those who knew the place of old. Bayham Abbey and Scotney Castle are famous places of interest very close by, whilst the village has its own commercial vineyard. Down the road is the hamlet of Hook Green with one of the most historic country pubs in the county – the Elephant's Head.

This walk takes you from the pub through open fields and alongside a river to one end of Lamberhurst where you enjoy a stroll the length of the main street. There is another pub to pop into if you can't wait to get back for a refill and the walk back takes you right through the vineyard with some lovely views across the Wealden countryside.

THE PUB THE ELEPHANT'S HEAD is a Harveys's tied house. Its distinctive design shows it was once a typical Wealden farmhouse which dates back to 1489 when it was owned by the abbot of nearby Bayham Abbey and was occupied by monks working the land. The building became a pub in 1768 and by 1795 it was known as the "Elephant Ale House", taking its current name in 1808. As befits its timber frame construction there are oak beams everywhere, a variety of cosy drinking and dining areas and a large open fireplace. There is a conservatory to the rear overlooking the garden with benches to the front. The pub had a substantial makeover in 2015. The menu changes daily. Ales from the Harveys range on our last visit were Olympia, Copper Wheat and Best.

⊕ www.elephants-head.co.uk. ☎ 01892 739525.

The Walk

❶ Turn right outside the pub car park and walk a short distance down the lane. Take the first footpath on the left, cross the field and keep going ahead until you reach a lane. Turn sharp left through the gate marked 'Furnace Mill' and then immediately sharp right to regain the footpath.

❷ Keep following this footpath as it bridges a stream and then skirts the left-hand side of a field. Keep ahead where the path emerges onto a concrete track, and then follow the path to the left. If you have crossed another bridge over a stream and are still on the concrete track you have gone too far. Keep along the path with the river on your right. You will pass a large barn on your left, keep going ahead.

❸ Where the path emerges onto the road, turn right. You now have a view down the main road of the village of Lamberhurst. On the left is the opportunity for another pub stop should you so wish. The Chequers

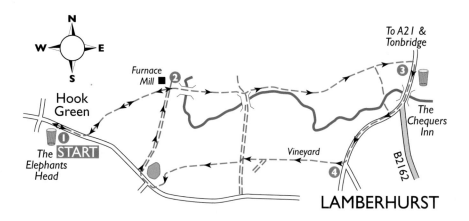

Inn is a quaint Kentish riverside pub which was originally a manor house in the 1100s, but has been a pub since the 15th century. It is said that Jane Austen was known to visit here. Traditional ales on offer on our last visit included Shepherd Neame Whitstable Bay and Master Brew Best. The pub also features a tea room and beer garden. Website: www.chequerslamberhurst.co.uk. The picturesque village has a whole host of interesting old buildings and is now quiet and tranquil thanks to the opening of a new bypass. Carry on along the main street. Take the right-hand fork. After the road has climbed up the hill, take the footpath on the right-hand side.

4 After you have climbed a few steps the path brings you out into Lamberhurst Vineyard. The vineyard, set amongst 20 acres of beautiful countryside, is one of the oldest in Kent. You can stop off for a guided tour and if two pubs aren't enough you can try tasting the wine! Keep going straight ahead along the footpath. Where the track veers to the left, follow the footpath straight ahead. Where it emerges onto a lane, turn left and then sharp right to the side of the barn. Keep following the path in the same direction. Where it enters the tree line, cross the stile, following it sharp left and then right. Cross the lane taking the path downhill on the other side until it finally emerges onto a road.

5 Turn right along the road for a short distance until the next track on the right, signposted for Furnace Mill. Turn right here and follow the track until you reach point 2 where you turn left and retrace your steps back to the start.

Place of Interest Nearby

Scotney Castle is actually two completely contrasting buildings – a Victorian country house and ruined moated castle, parts of which date from 1137. The original plan for the castle may never have been finished, and by 1558 it is likely only one tower remained. Around 1630 part of it was rebuilt in three-story Inigo Jones style but it was all partly demolished on the completion of the new house in 1843, leaving the ruin as a garden feature. The castle is set in one of England's most romantic 'picturesque' style gardens surrounded by a beautiful wooded estate.

The medieval bridge over the River Medway

Walk 8
EAST FARLEIGH

Distance: 3 miles (4.8 km)

Map: OS Explorer 148 Maidstone and the Medway Towns
GR: TQ735533

Dog notes: Along the river bank its best to keep your dog on a lead given the popularity of fishing.

How to get there: From the M20 junction 5 take the A20 eastbound and then immediately the B2246 through Barming. Cross the A26, keeping straight ahead the road drops down into East Farleigh. The Bull is on the left hand side up the hill having crossed the river.

Parking: The Bull Inn car park or off street parking in Vicarage Lane which is opposite the pub. **Postcode:** ME15 0HD.

East Farleigh is a small village located on the hillside surrounding the River Medway, south of Maidstone. The village appears in the *Doomsday Book* as *Feriaga*, from the Saxon word meaning a passage, in this case, over the river. There is a 12th-century parish church dedicated to Saint Mary which is opposite The Bull Inn from where we start our walk, one of three public houses in the parish.

The walk starts in the village, drops down to the river, crossing the historic bridge. You will enjoy a pleasant and picturesque riverside walk before a steady climb up the side of the valley with rewarding views back across the landscape which is dotted with orchards and oast houses before dropping back down into the village.

THE PUB **THE BULL INN** is a cosy wood panelled pub with a garden and play area for the summer and a real log fire for the winter. If you have a dog with you, there are a couple of designated tables inside where you can sit. A Sunday carvery is available from midday until it runs out! Real ales on tap when we visited were Harvey's Best and Sharp's Doom Bar.

⊕ www.thebulleastfarleigh.co.uk. ☎ 01622 726282.

The Walk:

❶ Turn right from the pub and walk to the bottom of Station Hill, crossing the historic bridge over the river.

❷ At the end of the bridge turn sharply to the left and follow the footpath signs down to the river. If you turn left at the river bank you can walk the short distance back underneath the bridge and take a look at the locks. However for the walk, turn right and keep following the footpath alongside the river. Follow the path until you reach the first bridge across the river. Turn left and cross the bridge.

❸ This is a charming riverside walk in an area famed for the chance to get a fleeting glimpse of a kingfisher skimming across the water – although we have never seen one! You are crossing Barming Bridge which is also known as the Kettle Bridge. Built in 1996, this modern metal bridge replaced an historic wooden one which gained some notoriety when part of it collapsed under the weight of a 10 ton traction engine. Having crossed the bridge carry on up the lane past the quaint cottages on either side of the road. At the end of the road turn right and then immediately left up the quiet and leafy Kettle Lane. After $^1/_3$ mile you will need to watch out for a footpath with a wooden kissing gate on the left which is quite hidden in the hedgerow. It's a short distance

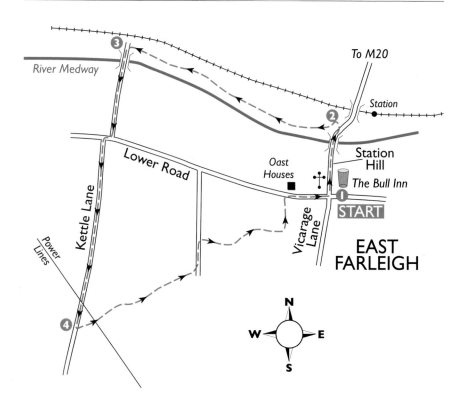

after you have passed beneath the electricity power line. If you end up back on a road you have missed the turn and need to go back.

④ Cross the field and follow the path into the woods. The path emerges into an orchard. Head forward but bear right through the orchard following the trodden path. Cross the access road and continue into the orchard ahead. The footpath emerges onto a lane down some steep steps in a hedgerow. Turn left down the lane and take the next signposted footpath on the right. Follow this through the woods and out through the fields until the end where it emerges onto a road opposite the group of oast houses. Turn right. The pub is a short distance along the road and you are back where you started.

Place of Interest on the Walk

The **bridge at East Farleigh** was built in the 14th century and is one of the oldest in Kent. There is no record of the date it was originally built but it was first mentioned in 1324. It provided the crossing point for Parliamentary forces in the Battle of Maidstone during the Civil War. Next to the bridge is a picturesque lock, one of several on this stretch of the River Medway. Thirty yards from the medieval bridge stands East Farleigh railway station which was built in the 1840s and still retains its original wooden South Eastern Railway station building and signal box.

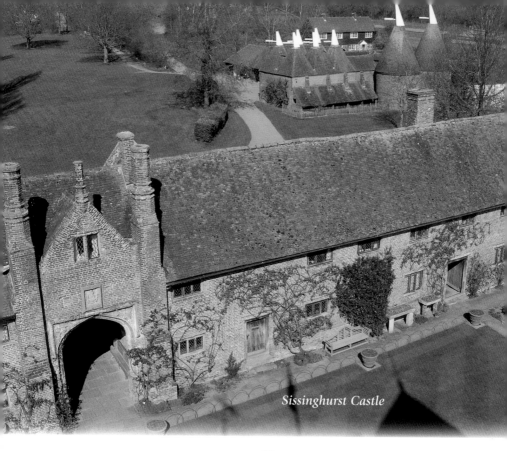

Sissinghurst Castle

Walk 9
SISSINGHURST

Distance: 3 miles (4.8 km)

Map: OS Explorer 136 The High Weald GR: TQ795373

How to get there: Sissinghurst is on the main A262 Lamberhurst to Biddenden road. The pub is on the left, in the middle of the village.

Parking: Outside the Milk House pub or in the pub car park. Postcode: TN17 2JG.

Originally referred to as Mylkehouse, or Milkhouse Street, Sissinghurst changed its name in the 1850s possibly to avoid association with the activities of the Hawkhurst Gang, an infamous group of smugglers who terrorised the surrounding areas and were feared by all along the south coast in the mid 1700s. Today, in contrast, it is a pretty village with picturesque buildings lining the main street with a relaxed and tranquil atmosphere.

This walk takes you in a large loop through fields, woods, lanes and tracks starting and finishing in the middle of the village right next to the pub.

THE PUB THE MILK HOUSE (referring to the village's previous name) is a former Kentish 16th-century hall which sports Tudor features yet has a modern and upmarket style. There is a large dining room and bar area. Outside, there is a spacious terrace with cushions available as added comfort for the furniture, and a hut where pizzas are freshly baked to order in a wood oven. A children's play area is set to the rear. Menus vary from a 'grazing'menu which offers a type of tapas selection or you can opt for the classic menu. The selection of ales on offer at the time of our visit included Harveys Best, Tonbridge Golden Rule and Old Dairy Gold Top. Open for teas, coffees and biscuits from 9am.
⊕ www.themilkhouse.co.uk. ☎ 01580 720200.

The Walk

1 Walk down the road opposite the pub (Chapel Lane) for a few yards and then take the footpath on the right. Keep to the right of the gate and turn left at the crossroads of paths. Follow the path out onto the field and keep going to the far side. As the path enters the tree line keep following it as it twists and turns through the woods, crossing a few streams in the process. Where it comes out into another field keep to the right-hand tree line and follow the path round to where it meets a road. Turn right onto the road and carry on until you reach the crossroads.

2 At the crossroads turn right along Golford Road for a few yards then take the track on the left. Follow it downhill keeping to the footpath ahead where the track diverges right through a gate. Follow it through the woods. Immediately after a small bridge with railings on the left-hand side of the path take the right-hand path out into the field. Keep following this path with the tree line on your right. You are heading to the right of the large farm buildings on the horizon.

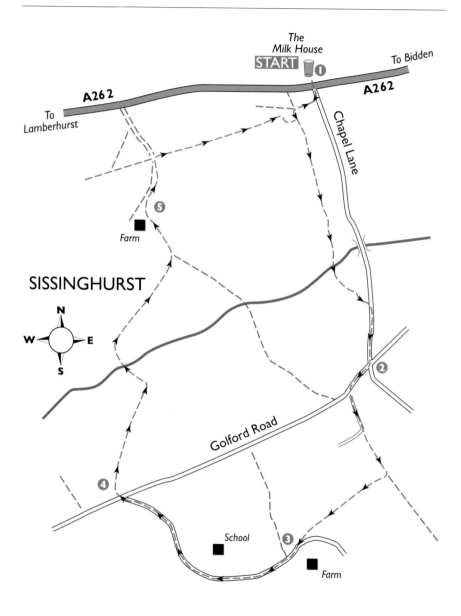

❸ When you exit the field and reach the buildings, bear right along the farm road. Now keep following this road ahead for just under ½ mile.

4 At a T-junction with a main road, take the farm track that bears right on the opposite side of the road. You now follow this track as it twists and turns in and out of the woods for another ½ mile. Where it finally peters out at the end of a field there is a footpath waymarker, follow it right through the gate. Cross the field – you are heading to the right of the house on the other side. Turn left, then sharp right, following the signs through the trees down into the farmyard where you turn right.

5 Follow the farm track where it climbs uphill. Where footpaths cross the lane turn right up the steps. Follow the path through the woods and out into the field. Follow the left-hand tree line until you are facing a fence. You will recognise this as you have re-joined the outward route. Retrace your steps by turning left, and then right at the footpath crossroads and you will be back on Chapel Lane.

Place of Interest Nearby

Sissinghurst Castle is a National Trust house and garden a couple of miles away. The garden is set in the ruin of an Elizabethan house in the middle of its own woods and farmland with long views across the Kentish landscape. The medieval manor house, which had been visited by Queen Elizabeth I, was restored by Vita Sackville-West, poet, novelist and gardener in the 1930's.

The Swale at the Harty Ferry

Walk 10

OARE

Distance: 4½ miles (7.2 km), extended version 5 miles (8 km).

Map: OS Explorer 149 Sittingbourne & Faversham **GR:** TR005629

How to get there: From the M2 follow the signs to Faversham. Then take the A2 in a westerly direction sign posted to Sittingbourne. Follow the signs to Oare. At the end of the B2045 turn left and park up immediately.

Parking: In the Three Mariners pub car park or in the village. **Postcode:** ME13 0QA.

Oare is a small village with a real maritime feel on the outskirts of Faversham right on the Saxon Shore Way long-distance footpath. The Oare Marshes Nature Reserve, managed by the Kent Wildlife Trust, consists of some 170 acres of mudflats and marshes. It is a wildlife haven for numerous wetland birds, both as a permanent habitat and as a migratory 'stopover'.

This is a contrasting walk, and one of our favourites, through one of the more remote parts of the county. It will take you through fields and then out onto the tidal reaches of The Swale, the channel of water separating Kent from the Isle of Sheppey. Part of the walk will be along part of the Saxon Shore Way. There is plenty of interest. The walk passes the nature reserve for much of its length whilst there are plenty of relics of Kent's maritime past dotted along the route.

THE PUB THE THREE MARINERS is a Grade II listed building right in the middle of the village which dates back to the late 18th century.

There is a bar and dining room with a split level terrace and garden at the rear looking out towards Oare Creek. From Mondays to Saturdays there is a very good value three course "Walkers Lunch" available with more expensive a la carte options. Ales on tap are from the Shepherd Neame stable – Spitfire Gold, Whitstable Pale Ale and Master Brew on our last visit.

⊕ www.thethreemarinersoare.co.uk. ☎ 01795 533633.

The Walk

1 From the pub car park turn right and follow Uplees Road through the village and out into the fields until it turns sharp right. At this point a footpath goes sharp left. It looks like a private drive but it is a right of way. Take the track across the field to the other side. When you reach the lane turn right and where the lane turns left, keep ahead along the track. Follow this track as far as you can. When you reach some buildings the path continues ahead to the right of the right-hand house. Keep ahead through the next gate then keep to the right-hand side of the field. Go through the next gate and to the exit from the following field which is around the telegraph poles visible on the far side. There is a footbridge over a stream midway across the field.

2 At the end of the field go through the gate, cross the track and take the footpath facing you. Follow this path between fields and you will come out at a gate to another lane. Cross the lane and keep straight ahead along the road opposite marked 'private road/public footpath'. Keep going in the same direction. The road peters out but the footpath

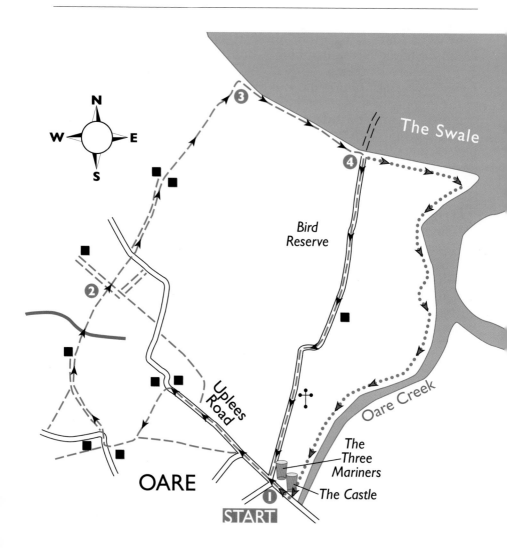

continues through some iron gates sandwiched between two cottages. Again keep going out onto the marshes. Just before the sea wall there are two metal gates, take the left-hand one. A short slope will bring you to the top of the sea wall. In front of you will be a small abandoned harbour known as Dan's Dock.

③ Go through the gate to the right of the old dock and keep following the path along the top of the sea wall. You are now on the Saxon Shore Way. On your left, just a short distance across the waters of the Swale, is the Isle of Sheppey. To your right is the Oare Marshes Nature Reserve, an area very popular with ornithologists. The reserve is of international importance for overwintering and migrating wetland birds. After a while you will see a car park on your right and you will cross a road which on your left-hand side disappears into the water. This was the Harty Ferry Road. The Harty Ferry was one of three ferries which linked mainland Kent with the Isle of Sheppey. Once the permanent crossing point at the Kings Ferry Bridge was established, the ferries fell out of use. The Harty Ferry ceased operation in 1946. There is a small visitor centre in the car park, usually open on weekends and bank holidays from 11am to 5pm.

4 Turn right down the lane and, passing the church on your left, follow the road back to the pub. Alternatively, you can take a slightly extended walk which carries on along the Swale on the Saxon Shore Way. Go straight ahead and there is a bird hide at the promontory where the path swings right, following Oare Creek where you will see a variety of boats, some in various stages of dereliction. Keep following the path alongside the creek. When you eventually reach the road turn right and after passing the Castle Inn, you will soon be back at the Three Mariners.

Place of Interest on the Walk

The whole area surrounding **Oare Marshes Nature Reserve** is a fascinating contrast of land and sea. Some of the green fields you walk through, although tranquil and remote now, were the site from 1787 until 1916 for the manufacture of gunpowder and the remains of a loading jetty at Dan's Dock is are still visible. The tidal mudflats of the Swale and Oare's own creek have their own nautical atmosphere. The Oare and Faversham Creeks are open for navigation at high tide. There is a history of shipbuilding and repair of historic boats and Thames Sailing Barges in the creeks.

Maritime contrasts seen from the walk alongside Oare Creek

Leeds Castle

Walk 11
LEEDS CASTLE

Distance: 3 miles (4.8 km)

Map: OS Explorer 137 Ashford **GR:** TQ838537

Dog notes: Dogs must be on a lead in the castle grounds. Despite an issue we had with an over keen member of the castle's security staff, the information boards at the entry points confirm that dogs are not banned from the public footpaths.

How to get there: From the M20 Junction 8, follow the signs to Lenham along the A20. The pub is a mile from the motorway on the right hand side of the road.

Parking: At the Park Gate Inn pub. **Postcode:** ME17 1PG.

Leeds Castle is advertised as the "loveliest castle in the world". It is certainly a fairy-tale sight attracting visitors from around the world. It comes with a history going back to the Norman conquest; later it was the home of six of England's medieval queens and in Tudor times

Henry VIII and his first wife Catherine of Aragon. By the 20th century it had become the ultimate country house retreat.

This walk takes you through part of the castle's 500 acre parkland where you can enjoy, close at hand, views of the iconic castle and its associated historic buildings. Please note you will be walking on public footpaths through private grounds. This walk keeps you on the public right of way where you can walk without charge, but if you wish to explore further, you should pay the admission fee. In order to avoid any confusion we have included the official footpath numbers on the map.

THE PARK GATE INN is named after the gate that once led into Leeds Castle Park in the mid 19th century. Park Gate was a small hamlet at that time and was served by the inn that has a 16th-century building at its centre. Although next to a main road, the pub has rustic charm with a brick fire place, beamed ceilings and various nooks and crannies. A pleasant beer garden sits to the side and rear for al fresco dining and drinking. There is a daily specials board. Ales available on our last visit were Sharp's Doom Bar, Greene King Old Speckled Hen, Black Sheep Best and Shepherd Neame Spitfire. The pub is open from midday until 11pm, last food orders are 9pm.
☎ 01622 880985.

The Walk

❶ Turn left out of the pub and follow the grass verge alongside the road for a short distance until you come to the first footpath on the left. Take this path and follow it through the trees, then across the golf course, then keep ahead and, following the yellow post, carry on over a tarmac track and into some trees. When you emerge from the trees cross over the tarmac path and keep ahead along the tarmac path facing you. Cross the bridge. When you get to the end (with a very old tree on your left) bear left and then immediately right, taking the unmade footpath up towards the gate.

❷ Just before the gate there is a concrete footpath sign at ground level. Go through the gate up the hill to the right of the big tree clump. You will soon be facing another gate; here bear left following the waymarker, keeping the fence on your right. Carry on up the slight hill. Where the

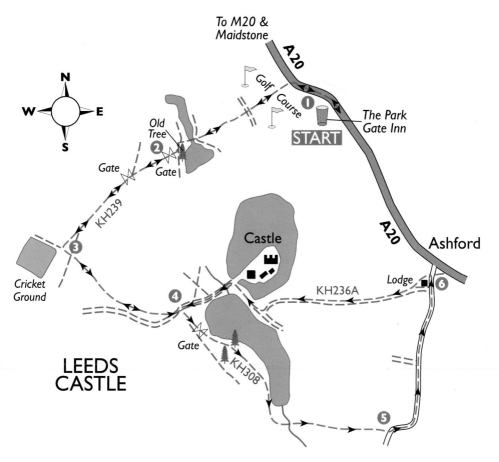

broad paths diverge, keep right into the trees (this is necessary to keep you on the public right of way).

3 When you emerge from the trees and you are facing a gate into a small cricket pitch, turn sharp left through the trees back into the grounds of the park. Look downhill towards the tarmac drive to the right of an isolated tree and you will see a yellow marker post indicating the right of way. Where the tarmac drive enters the trees go through the gate noting the direction of the waymarker.

4 After you have passed a small service car park on the right, turn right off the tarmac drive immediately after the bushes. A yellow waymarker

points the way. Now go across the grass following the next waymarker and down the slight gradient. At the fence line at the bottom the right of way goes through the left-hand gate. With good views of the castle on your left cross the tiny bridge over the brook and head up the path between the trees. Carry on in the same direction taking the path through the gate into the woods. Cross the stream and continue along the path until it emerges onto a lane.

5 Turn left up the lane, following it uphill for a little while.

6 A few yards before the lane joins a main road take the signposted footpath on the left. Drop down the steps and bear left at the bottom. Turn right along the tarmac drive and follow it to the very end. Yellow waymarkers confirm this is a right of way. With the castle very close by across the moat, turn right at the end. When the castle entrance over a bridge is on your right, turn left to face the remains of the barbican. There is a concrete public footpath sign pointing the way at ground level. Now follow this tarmac path very slightly uphill. Don't bear right. Another ground-level footpath sign confirms the way. You will shortly be at point 4, then retrace your steps back to the start.

Place of Interest on the Walk

Leeds Castle gets its name from the manor of Esledes. Construction of the first stone castle began in 1119. The area surrounding the castle was carefully designed and included raised viewing points from which the building could be seen at its best. In 1278 the castle was bought by the wife of Edward I and remained in Royal hands until Tudor times. It was later owned by some of the most influential families in the country such as the Culpeppers in the 17th century and Fairfaxes in the 18th century. In 1926 it was bought by an Anglo-American heiress, later to become Lady Baillie, who undertook extensive renovations before leaving the castle to a charitable trust that is now responsible for its preservation.

The view across one of the lakes between points 4 and 5 on the walk

The Archbishop's Palace in the village centre

Walk 12

CHARING

Distance: 3 miles (4.8 km)

Map: OS Explorer 137 Ashford GR: TQ 949514

Dog Notes: This walk is not suitable for a dog you cannot assist over a stile.

How to get there: Charing village is on the A20 about 5 miles east of Junction 9. From the village follow the A20 in the direction of Maidstone. Once you have crossed the large roundabout on the outskirts of the village, after a mile take the first right hand turn signposted to Stalisfield Green. Just keep going ahead and uphill and the pub will appear to your right after another mile.

Parking: At the Bowl Inn pub. Postcode: TN27 0HG.

Charing is an ancient village which sits in the shadow of the North Downs. For centuries it has been a place for travellers to stop and rest. It was one of the last stopping points on the Pilgrims' Way to Canterbury.

This walk takes you from the heights of the downs into the village along a mix of footpaths and quiet country lanes including a short stretch along the ancient Pilgrims' Way. There is plenty to see, including marvellous sweeping views from the top of the hill, past a windmill and the historic village itself.

THE PUB **THE BOWL INN** is situated in quite a remote spot but remains resolutely popular. Its slightly austere exterior hides its 16th-century origins; it was originally built as a farmhouse in 1512, becoming a brewhouse in 1606. Inside it has been extensively refurbished with a large dining area circling a central fireplace. The bar is to one side and features the ability to serve beers through the front window to customers seated outside. The menu is varied, everything from pub classics to sandwiches, baguettes and ploughmans. Ales on tap on our last visit were Wantsum Ravening Wolf, Old Dairy Red Top and Westerham Bulldog. There is a large garden to the rear.
⊕ www.bowlinncharing.com. ☎ 01233 712256.

The Walk

1 Outside the pub turn left along the lane. Take the first footpath on the right. It is at a dip in the lane just before a gated drive marked Tangle Wood and is not signposted. Follow this path through the woods to the end. Cross the next lane, the path is immediately opposite and again is not signed – it is only marked by a hole in the hedge. Once you are through the hedge the path is clearly apparent. Carry on to the far side of the field. Cross the road and again the path continues immediately on the other side by a post.

2 Follow the path around the buildings and when you emerge into a field on the hillside take the path through a small gap in the trees to your left. Follow it up to a stile, cross the stile and at the field bear left towards a windmill. You are heading for a stile slightly to the right of the windmill. Cross the stile and then bear immediately right keeping the scrub and tree line to your right. Follow the path down to the far corner and into the trees. Now keep along the path as it

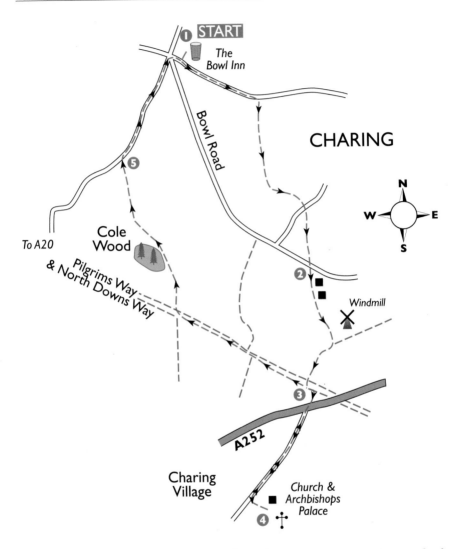

drops downhill. At the bottom where it emerges onto a tarmacked track turn left.

3 A few yards later turn right and keep ahead across the main road. You are now entering Charing village. After a few hundred yards, in the middle of the village, turn left along the drive signposted for the church.

4 The church will be facing you and the remains of the Archbishop's Palace will be on your left. Now retrace your steps to point 3 and keep going ahead along the track which is waymarked in red as the North Downs Way. This is also the ancient Pilgrims' Way, the historic route taken by pilgrims from Winchester and London, to the shrine of Thomas Becket at Canterbury. The route closely follows a pre-existing ancient trackway dated by archaeological finds to 500–450 BC but it has probably been in existence since the Stone Age. Where the paths diverge, take the lower route with a red waymarker. At the next crossing of paths turn right taking the path up the steps and then uphill across the field. This can be indistinct, but you are heading to the immediate right-hand side of the large wood (Cole Wood) at the top of the field slightly to the left. When you reach the top a yellow waymarker confirms the route through a gap in the hedge line. Take a few minutes to turn back and admire the stunning view from this part of the North Downs. With Charing village and church now beneath you, on a clear day you can see to the very tip of the Kent coast marked by the rectangular blocks of the power stations at Dungeness. Continue across the next field. At the other side another waymarker confirms the route across the following field.

5 At the end turn right along the lane. After ¹/₃ mile the pub will be on the right.

Place of Interest on the Walk

The **Archbishop's Palace** was one of three medieval palaces, the others being Otford and Croydon, serving the archbishops and their retinue when they travelled between Canterbury and London. It was in regular use from the time of Archbishop Peckham (1279–1292), although the present buildings date mostly from the 14th century. Henry VIII stayed at the palace on his way to meet the king of France at the Field of the Cloth of Gold. The property was seized by the Crown after the Dissolution in 1545. It became a working farm, with the buildings turned into a farmhouse, a couple of cottages, and animal accommodation, and the great hall turned into a barn. It is now a Grade I listed building. Adjacent to the palace is the parish church of St Peter and St Paul. The church's west tower was built in the 14th century, though most of the rest of the building was reconstructed following a catastrophic fire in the 16th century.

The view from the walk looking back towards Charing village

Appledore village

Walk 13
APPLEDORE

Distance: 7 miles (11.2 km)

Map: OS Explorer: 125 Romney Marsh, Rye & Winchelsea.
GR: TQ941286

How to get there: From the M20 at Ashford follow the A2070 to Brenzett, at the roundabout take the third exit. As soon as you reach Appledore take the left hand turn immediately after you have crossed the canal. At the end of that road turn left and the pub is a short distance on the left.

Parking: Opposite the Ferry Inn pub. Postcode: TN30 7JY.

Appledore is a quiet village with many old houses lining its unusually wide main street. The name Appledore comes from the Old English apuldre (meaning apple tree) and is first recorded in the 10th century. Appledore was once a port on the estuary of the River Rother. Famously, the greater part of the Danish army of 280 ships wintered here in 892 AD, before moving into Wessex and suffering defeat at the hands of the Saxons. The importance of Appledore as a port diminished suddenly in the 13th century when storms caused the river Rother to change its course. The wide village street with its Tudor and Georgian houses now leads down to the Royal Military Canal

This is a walk rich in variety that will take you alongside some of the water channels that are a distinctive feature of Romney Marsh. You will pass through the attractive village itself, which is well off the tourist trail, and then spend some time following the meanders of the Royal Military Canal, one of the major defences of England built to counter the threat of Napoleonic invasion. Ancient Kenardington Church is visited before returning back through fields and vineyards.

THE FERRY INN is a 17th-century free house that was the home of the ferry between the Isle of Oxney and the English mainland at Appledore. All the flat land around here was once beneath the sea until it was reclaimed to become the fertile Romney Marsh. The high ground of the Isle of Oxney was then a real island rising out of it. The pub offers a variety of inside dining areas with tables outside. It can get very busy on Sunday lunchtimes. There is an extensive specials board. Real ales on offer on our last visit were Harveys Best, Sharps Doom Bar, Three Legs Pale Ale and Oxney ale, a house beer brewed by Goachers of Maidstone. ⊕ www.oxneyferry.com. ☎ 01233 758 246.

The Walk

1 With your back to the Ferry Inn turn right, cross the bridge and turn sharp right. You are now on the Saxon Shore Way. After a mile it will climb a hillock. On the other side cross the stile, walk down the steps and at the road turn right. Walk to the end of the road.

2 Appledore church will be facing you, set back from the road behind some cottages. It dates from the early 13th century with some 14th-century additions. At the end of the road turn right, and then left along the path before the bridge. Continue alongside the canal for 1¾ miles, for most of the distance there is both a narrow path on top of the ridge closer to the water and a lower broader path. The lower path is what remains of the Royal Military Road. On the way note the pillbox hidden behind the bank – the Napoleonic defences had another potential airing in World War II.

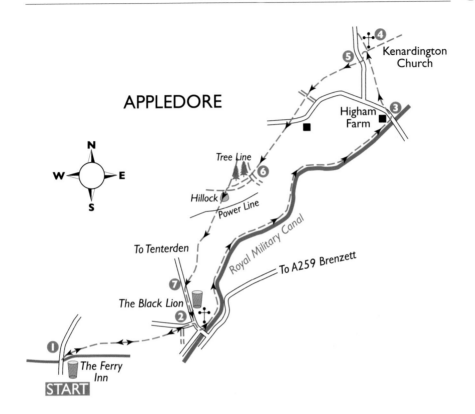

APPLEDORE

Kenardington
Church

Higham
Farm

Tree Line

Hillock

Power Line

Royal Military Canal

To Tenterden

To A259 Brenzett

The Black Lion

The Ferry
Inn

START

❸ At the first road you come to, go through the gate and turn left. After a
short distance you pass Higham Farm on the left, then take the footpath
on the right. Follow this path steadily uphill for approximately half a
mile until you come to Kenardington church. (On our last visit which
was in mid-summer just before harvest, the field approaching the
church was planted with crops which were dense and rose to adult
head height. It was quite arduous to get through. Shorter children
would not be able to see where they were going and might find it
distressing. An alternative route would be to keep going straight up
the lane at point 3 and not turn off.) Follow the path through the tree
line into the churchyard. St Mary's church stands on the site of what
is believed to be a small Saxon fort. It is recorded in the Domesday
Book when an annual fee of a shilling was paid to the monks of
Christchurch, Canterbury. This indicates that it is likely the monks
were the original founders of the church. The tower dates from 1170

and is a square structure without buttresses. To the north side is an unusual round tower, which carries the staircase to the belfry at the top of the main tower.

4 Retrace your steps out of the churchyard and turn immediately right when you emerge from the tree line. You will now be following the Saxon Shore Way all the way back to the start of the walk. Follow the path as it turns quickly left and right around the field boundary until you pass through a gate onto a lane.

5 Turn left and a few yards later take the path on the right. It's quite hidden, just before a telegraph pole. You will now continue along this path for a mile. On the way keep ahead when you cross a sunken lane and emerge into a vineyard. At the end of the vineyard drop down the steps and turn right then quickly left back onto the path. Again there is another vineyard, just keep going in the same direction, always following the Saxon Shore Way.

⑥ When you cross a farm track the path bears slightly right on the other side of the tree line. For a short while now the path will be a farm track with the tree line next to you on the right. After a short while you will see an unusual hillock ahead of you, slightly to your left. The path actually goes over the top of it. Follow it over and keep going ahead down the other side underneath the power lines with yet another vineyard on your left. Go through the gate at the bottom and go straight across the next field. Cross the stream. In the next field the path is indistinct. Just cross the field keeping straight ahead and at the other side turn left keeping the hedge line on your right. There is another Saxon Shore Way waymarker in the hedge to keep you in the right direction. Keep to the right of the field with the houses on your right. When you get to a tarmac track turn right and go through the gate on your right. Once through the gate bear immediately left diagonally across the recreation ground, the path officially emerges onto the road to the left of the toilets.

⑦ Once on the road, turn left and follow it down the main street to point 2. On the right you'll pass Miss Mollett's Tea Rooms. Light lunches and afternoon tea with home-made cakes are on offer. Website: www. missmollettstearoom.co.uk. Tel 01233 758555 to check for opening times. At point 2 turn right and retrace your steps back to the start. If you are gasping for an early pint the Black Lion is on your left.

Place of Interest on the Walk

The **Royal Military Canal** is a canal running for 28 miles between Seabrook near Hythe and Cliff End near Fairlight. It was built as a defence against the possible invasion of England during the Napoleonic Wars. Construction started in 1804. Civilian navvies dug the canal itself, while soldiers built the ramparts. Up to 1,500 men were employed in the project. You may notice that the canal frequently gently zig zags - gun batteries were placed where the canal was staggered, this would give defending troops a clear line of sight to shoot down the next stretch of water. A military road was built on the inland side of the canal, this now forms the broader lower path below the overgrown ramparts along which the narrower path runs along the top of the ridge. The canal never saw any active military use and became something of a white elephant; it is now – literally – a sleepy backwater.

Lympne Castle

Walk 14
LYMPNE

Distance: 5 miles (8 km) or 7 miles (11.2 km) for the extended version.

Map: OS Explorer 138 Dover Folkestone & Hythe GR: TR120333

How to get there: From the M20 Junction 11 take the A20 to Newingreen and keep straight ahead for Lympne. At the far end of the road turn left then first right. Drop down the hill through West Hythe and keep following the lane. The pub will be on the left hand side.

Parking: At or outside the Botolphs Bridge Inn. **Postcode:** CT21 4NL.

In Roman times Lympne was known as Portus Lemanis, it lay at the end of the Roman road from Canterbury, known today as Stone Street. It had a Saxon Shore fort, its remains are at the bottom of the south-facing cliffs. In the 13th century a castle was established at the top of the cliff line, it was restored in the early years of the 20th century and more recently a wildlife park and zoo has been established in the landscape.

This walk is the most strenuous in the book but it rewards you with a truly diverse itinerary. You start across the flat landscape of Romney Marsh, take a canal-side walk past the remains of the Roman fort then climb what used to be sea cliffs to arrive at Lympne, home to the castle, ancient church and some truly amazing views. You might even get a peek at the zoo animals through the fence! Try to take this walk on a clear day to make the most of the vistas on offer.

THE PUB The BOTOLPHS BRIDGE INN, sitting next to one of the watercourses on Romney Marsh takes its name from local legend. It concerns the English monk St Botolph who lived in the 7th century and the pub sign tells the story. There is a boat, with a coffin, like an ark, being carried by monks from the river bank, and a shaft of light is seen shining down on them from a black sky. The legend is that the body of St Botolph was being taken to a place where it would be kept safe from desecration by the heathen Danes. There was water to cross, and the night was pitch black. Suddenly a shaft of light shone down from heaven to guide them as they went on their way. Today the pub offers an extensive menu – light bites with a full evening menu. Available ales on our visit were Sharps Doom Bar and Greene King IPA. The pub is closed Mondays except bank holidays. ⊕ www.botolphsbridgeinn.co.uk. ☎ 01303 267346.

The Walk

1 From the pub cross the bridge and bear left along the leafy lane. After a few twists and turns it becomes residential before crossing the Royal Military Canal over a bridge.

2 Immediately after the bridge turn left and walk alongside the canal, either along the narrow upper path or broad lower road. Once you have passed a dam on the left make sure you drop down to the lower track as on the right-hand side there is a viewing point for the remains of the Roman Port Lemanis. Also known as Stutfall Castle, this was the site chosen in the early 2nd century AD as a base for the Roman naval fleet in British waters. The fort here was built around 265 AD but because its remains have been displaced by landslips, its shape is difficult to decipher. It was abandoned by the late 4th century. A short

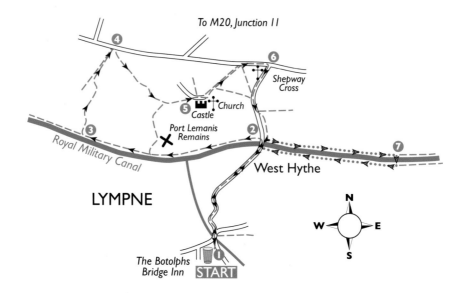

distance later on the right is a path heading up the hillside, this is not part of the walk but if you go along it you will get a different view of the Roman remains. Carry on along the canal-side path. On your right you might get a glimpse of some of the residents of the wildlife park behind the fence.

3 Now take the next right-hand turn, waymarked a bridle path and footpath HE 317. It's a long and steady climb to the top. These were once the sea cliffs before the water receded and Romney Marsh was created and where you have just walked would have been the shoreline. The climb to the top is fairly steep in places but reward yourself by occasionally turning round and taking in the view. Where the path becomes an abandoned tarmac lane, bear right up the hill.

4 At the top take the footpath on the right just before the main road. You now just follow this ahead, initially through woods and later where the landscape opens up on the right to reveal a stunning panorama of Romney Marsh and the English Channel with the coastline curving around to the top of Dungeness and in the far distance the cliffs at Fairlight. Take a seat on the bench where this section of trees has been adopted as 'Millennium Wood', a simple but effective memorial to a local resident where individual types of tree have been identified.

5 Continuing ahead the route passes some buildings and then bears left up a drive into a lane. At the end turn right then bear left (not sharp left) at the courtyard facing you and carry on along the lane with the courtyard wall on your right. You will now be at the entrance to Lympne Castle. Take a peek through the entrance arch on your right then go through the gate into the churchyard of the 12th-century parish church of St Stephen. It's worth taking a circuit around the church for more views on the far side of the churchyard. Leaving the churchyard the way you came in, turn sharp right along the broad lane. At the end of the lane turn right along the road. A short distance later you will arrive at the Shepway Cross.

6 From the cross turn right down the lane. About half way down there is a footpath on the left by a garage. Ignore this but take the footpath a few yards further down on the left behind the brick wall. You can follow this path down to West Hythe away from the lane. You are back at point 2. Either return to the start, or for an extended walk turn left before the bridge along the canal. A mile later there is a footbridge across it.

7 Turn right over the bridge and right again along the path on the other side of the canal. This will bring you back to point 2 after a mile. Turn left and follow the outward route back to the start.

Place of Interest on the Walk

Lympne Castle dates from the 13th century and was once occupied by Thomas Becket. It forms a fortified manor house associated with the neighbouring 12th-century **St Stephen's Church**. The site's high vantage point makes both buildings stand out on the skyline. During Tudor times the castle was rented as a farmhouse but in the 19th century it was left to decay. The castle was bought in 1905 by Sir Richard Lorimer and was restored. During the restoration the original buildings were extended and modern buildings were incorporated into the castle. It remains privately owned, used mainly for weddings and corporate events.

A glance into Lympne Castle at point 5 on the walk

Whitstable Harbour

Walk 15
WHITSTABLE

Distance: 2 miles (3.2 km), 3 miles (4.8 km) for the extended version.

Map: OS Explorer 150 Canterbury & Thanet **GR:** TR103664

How to get there: From the main A299 follow the signs for Whitstable. Go through the town centre, (it may get congested in summer). After the short one way section turn right down Cromwell Road and then left into the car park.

Parking: None whatsoever at the pub – that's why we start this walk from the town car park. **Postcode: CT5 1LB.**

Whitstable has become the most popular resort in Kent in recent years. It's a town of contrasts with ancient buildings, a working harbour, upmarket restaurants, fish and chip shops, beaches and the nearby rolling clifftop at Tankerton. For pubs you are really spoilt for choice.

There is so much to see and do in the town; we have devised a walk to take in just about all of it in a fairly short circuit. You will walk along some of the quaint side streets and take in the beach and the bustling harbour, and take a bracing stroll up on Tankerton Slopes with some great views out to sea. The problem is which pub to base it on. On the walk we estimated at least a dozen were either on, or a very short distance from the route.

So we've opted for a Whitstable institution, the **OLD NEPTUNE**, known locally as the 'Neppy'. Its fame is down to its location – it's actually on the beach which also serves as its beer garden. The current pub dates from 1897 after its predecessor was completely washed away in a storm. It was rebuilt using timber reclaimed from the original structure and several other cottages that had also been destroyed. The building has warped and twisted over the years owing to its old wooden foundations. Take a look at the crazy angle of the bar which drops down towards the floor. It certainly has a unique atmosphere, however its location means that road access is extremely limited so for this walk we've started at one of the town's car parks. For food it has pub favourites with daily seafood specials. On sunny days during the summer a barbecue serves burgers and hotdogs directly from the beach. Ales on our last visit were Goldings Summer Ale and (aptly) Whitstable Bay from Shepherd Neame and Harveys Best. ⊕ www.thepubonthebeach.co.uk. ☎ 01227 272262.

The Walk

❶ Walk out of the car park into Cromwell Road and turn right. At the end of Cromwell Road, turn left into Harbour Street and keep right, on the other side of the railings, into Sea Street, keeping right into Sea Wall. The town's backstreets and alleyways served as convenient escape routes for smugglers, as Whitstable was, like most Kentish coastal towns, awash with the illegal trade in tobacco and spirits, as well as people, during the Napoleonic wars. The wooden fishermen's sheds now fetch premium prices for residential use. Continue along Sea Wall passing the Pearson's Arms on your right.

❷ When you emerge onto a crossroads with Middle Wall ahead of you, turn right along Terry's Lane. This will immediately become Island Wall. On the right-hand side you will see the fishing boat 'Favourite'

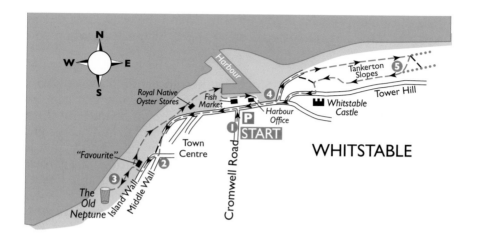

moored high and dry between the cottages. Built in 1890 she is the last oyster yawl to remain in Whitstable. She commemorates the town's oyster fishing and shipbuilding industries. In the 19th century there would have been 100 similar boats at sea at any one time. She was beached in 1952 near the site of shipyards, sail makers and forges that once thrived on the shoreline. Next to the boat turn right down Starboard Light Alley and left onto the seafront. You will see the Old Neptune in front of you.

3 From The Old Neptune, retrace your steps back along either the beach or the seafront path. Note the eclectic variety of houses and cottages fronting the beach. Keep to the shore side of the Royal Native Oyster Stores building and carry on towards the harbour. Oysters are synonymous with the town. In some years, up to half the oysters sold in London came from Whitstable. Farming oysters is a better description than fishing as the oysters may need to be sown on the sea bed, checked annually, and predators such as starfish removed before the four- or five-year-old oysters are harvested. Bear right along the bustling harbour side and follow it to the far end. Leave the harbour next to the harbour office and, on the road, bear left and then turn left into Beach Walk at the bottom of the hill.

4 Follow Beach Walk onto the seafront and then keep left along the promenade. At the end of the rows of beach huts, take the first path on the right, up the hillside. At the top bear right and head for the ship's mast and cannon. If you want to extend the walk, continue at the lower level and retrace your steps at the higher level when you choose to.

5 You are now on Tankerton Slopes with commanding views across the Thames estuary and the North Sea. On a clear day you can see the World War II Maunsell sea forts on the horizon behind the wind farm. Continue past the benches and take the footpath that bears right into the clump of trees. Follow it down and then up. Shortly after it emerges from the woods, take the path on the left through the garden and out onto the road. Opposite and to the left is Whitstable Castle. The 'castle' used to be Whitstable's manor house, the oldest part being built in the 1790s. It was later used as local government offices with the panelled billiard room transformed into the council chamber. The

building has been restored over the last few years, the grounds are now a public park and teas are served inside. Returning down the road will bring you out at point 4 with the start of the walk a short distance on the left-hand side.

Place of Interest on the Walk

Whitstable harbour was built in 1832 by the Canterbury and Whitstable Railway Company in order to transport goods from the sea to Canterbury. It remains very much a working harbour with an aggregate terminal. Fishing and fish processing being the main activities. The harbour-side fish markets are popular with both residents and visitors; one of the largest has its own restaurant above it guaranteeing the freshest produce. In the summer there are stands and stalls which pop up serving all manner of fresh traditional seafood, including of course the famous oysters.

Sunset at Whitstable Bay where the walk passes the harbour near point 4

The beach at Reculver

Walk 16
RECULVER

Distance: 4½ miles (7.2 km)

Map: OS Explorer 150 Canterbury & Isle of Thanet **GR:** TR226692

How to get there: From the main A299 east of Herne Bay follow the signs to Reculver. Carry on past the caravan parks to the very end of the road. The pub will be on the right and the car park on the left.

Parking: Car park opposite the King Ethlebert pub. The fee was a very reasonable £1 all day at the time of writing. **Postcode:** CT6 6SU.

Reculver is one of the most prominent features on the Kent Coast. The towers of the former church have been a guide for mariners for centuries, whilst the area is steeped in Roman history.

This walk takes you through the historic remains and out into the marshes before doubling back to the sea wall for an easy shore-line walk on the return.

THE PUB THE KING ETHELBERT is certainly a pub with a location – right in the shadow of the towers and with the Roman walls of Reculver's fort almost touching the building. The walls of the bar are covered with pictures of the area's past. There is a deck outside. The menu mainly features pub classics but sandwiches and baguettes are also available. Ales on tap on our visits have been Ripple Steam Best, Caledonian Flying Scotsman and Fullers London Pride. The pub is open all day every day.
☎ 01227 374368.

The Walk

❶ Turn right outside the pub and follow the path up past the towers and down the other side. Turn left at the bottom and then right onto the sea wall. With the shellfish hatchery in front of you, turn immediately

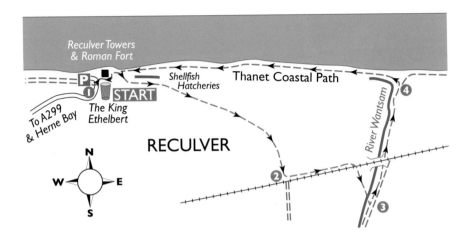

right through the gate following the waymarker. With the hatchery on your left, continue along the embankment. Continue for a mile until you reach the railway line.

2 Do not cross the railway at the first crossing. Turn left and continue along the embankment with the railway on your right. About $^1/_3$ mile mile later, go over the railway at the next crossing you come to. As always, exercise extreme care when crossing the tracks. Stop, look and listen. Follow the path to the end and cross the river Wantsum. This small channel is all that remains of a broad expanse of water known as the Wantsum Channel which separated Thanet, when it was a real island, from the rest of Kent. The low ground on which you have been walking was under water. One of the reasons for establishing a Roman fort at Reculver was to guard this channel of water.

3 Turn left up onto the track and walk back along it in the direction of the railway. Cross the tracks again and at the other side continue in the same direction. Immediately after you have crossed the line there will be a quick zigzag left then right, then keep ahead in the direction of the sea wall.

4 At the end of the path turn left along the concrete path following the sea wall. Continue along this path, passing the towers, all the way back to the start.

Place of Interest on the Walk

Reculver Tower and Roman Fort is the site of the Roman settlement and fort "Regulbium" dating back to 43 AD. Much of the Roman wall survives and is best seen around the east side of the site which you will notice on your return leg of the walk. In the 7th century a monastery was built in the remains of the fort. It was a seat of the Anglo-Saxon kings – hence the name of the pub. The towers are 12th-century additions to all that remain of the once magnificent Anglo-Saxon church of St Mary. Coastal erosion claimed much of the village which the church served and most of it was demolished around 1805. The towers, known as the 'Twin Sisters', had become an important landmark for mariners so were preserved by Trinity House in 1810 as an aid to navigation. This coastline has a place in modern history too. This was where the famous 'Dambusters' 617 Squadron tested their 'bouncing bombs' which in 1943 were used to destroy dams in the German Ruhr district at the height of World War II.

The remains of St Mary's church

Fordwich town

Walk 17
FORDWICH

Distance: 3 miles (4.8 km)

Map: OS Explorer 150 Canterbury and Isle of Thanet GR: TR180597

Dog notes: This walk is not suitable if you have a dog you cannot assist over a cattle grid.

How to get there: From Canterbury, take the A28 in the direction of Margate. The turn for Fordwich is 2 miles from the city centre on the right hand side. When you reach Fordwich, after the road turns sharp left, keep straight ahead and the pub is on the left hand side.

Parking: Outside the Fordwich Arms pub. Postcode: CT2 0DB.

Fordwich is a picturesque settlement situated at what was once the limit of navigation on the River Stour. It became the port for Canterbury where stone to build the cathedral was landed from Normandy. The town hall, built around 1544, is the oldest

and smallest in the country still in use by a current town council.

Fordwich is a relatively unknown gem. This walk takes you out of the town, initially alongside the River Stour and then through woods, open heathlands and fields, and back into the town.

THE PUB As the picture shows, **THE FORDWICH ARMS** sits snugly between the church and the old timber-framed town hall. It features a bar and lounge with a real manor house feel. There is a separate oak-panelled dining room with a covered terrace next to the river and a large pleasant garden at the rear. Ales such as Sharps Atlantic, Otter Ale and Adnam's Ghostship were on offer at the time of our visit. Menus change daily.

⊕ www.fordwicharms.co.uk.☎ 01227 710444.

The Walk

1 Turn left from the pub and then (with the church on your left) right, into the town. Keep ahead where the busier road joins on the left and follow the road around the corner. Take the footpath on the left just before the bridge. Keep ahead along this path (which is also a cycle trail) firstly across open meadows and then through woodland. After 1 mile you will pass a fishing lake on your left.

2 Shortly after the lake, at a fork in the path, take the left path. Continue uphill with the path curving to the left and out onto the open heathland. Carry on a short distance until you come to a gravel track. Turn left onto the track and follow it through the fenced gap of an

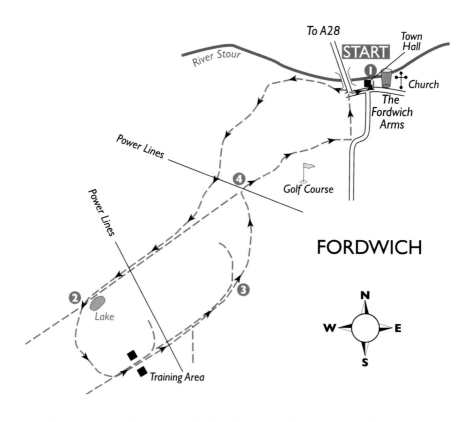

assault course. Keep following this track and where there is a fork keep ahead on the track over the first cattle grid.

3 A short distance after a second cattle grid the track curves left. You now keep ahead along the less defined path and you will soon have gorse bushes on both sides. Follow this path as it drops down and then enters woodland. Follow it through the woods.

4 When you have an electricity pylon in front of you above the trees and the main path swings left, keep right along the less-used path. Then turn immediately right through the gap in the wooden sleepers following the yellow waymarker. The path soon crosses a golf course. Follow the white posts as the path re-enters the woods slightly to the left of the second post. When you emerge from the wood, cross the field and at the far side turn left at the field line. Follow this path ahead all the way back down to the town. When you are facing the river bridge again, turn right, back to the start.

Place of Interest on the Walk

Fordwich became a corporate limb of the Cinque Ports in 1050. Henry II granted the town a charter in 1184 allowing self-government and exemption from taxes. The town hall is directly opposite the pub. The ground floor was the town gaol and the last time prisoners were held here was in 1885 when three men had been caught poaching trout. In the courtroom upstairs, criminal cases were tried until 1886. The town hall is open on Sundays and bank holiday Monday afternoons from May-September and every Wednesday during August. Every year since 1292, Fordwich has elected a mayor.

Bourne House

Walk 18
BISHOPSBOURNE

Distance: 2 miles (3.2 km)

Map: OS Explorer 150 Canterbury and Isle of Thanet **GR:** TR190524

How to get there: From the A2 south of Canterbury take the exit for Bishopsbourne. When you reach the bottom of the hill turn left and the pub will be on your right. From the A2 from Dover again follow the signs but turn right at the bottom of the hill.

Parking: Outside the Mermaid pub. **Postcode:** CT4 5HX.

Bishopsbourne is a tiny, archetypal English village south of Canterbury. Once part of the grand Bourne Park Estate there is a church, manor house, a few quiet cottages spread around the leafy lanes and of course – the village pub. Bishopsbourne has been included by *The Times* in their list of 20 best villages in the South of England.

This short walk takes you through the little-known and unspoilt countryside of the Elham Valley. It's a gentle meander through the fields – perhaps ideal for working off a Sunday lunch!

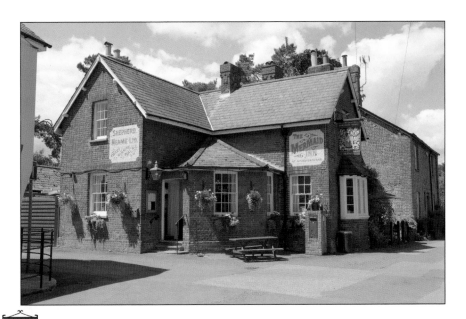

THE PUB THE MERMAID is a small red brick village pub and was built in 1861. But why the name so far from the sea? Originally called the Lion's Head, the pub was built to serve local estate workers, until it was bought, along with the Bourne Park estate, by an industrialist in the 1920s. The name was changed to The Mermaid Inn as the mythical creature featured on the new owners coat of arms. There are separate bar and dining areas and a bench outside were you can take in the peace and tranquillity of this secluded spot. The menu is extensive; from light lunches of warm ciabattas and Kentish cheese ploughmans to full a la carte. Ales on tap on our last visit were Shepherd Neame Master Brew and Spitfire Gold.
⊕ www.mermaidinnbishopsbourne.co.uk. ☎ 01227 830 581.

The Walk

❶ Turn sharp left outside the pub and walk up the lane to the crossroads opposite the church.

❷ At the crossroads turn right and walk a little distance up the lane. Turn left by the cottage and take the footpath on the immediate right behind it. Walk up the hill to the end of the footpath. On your left you

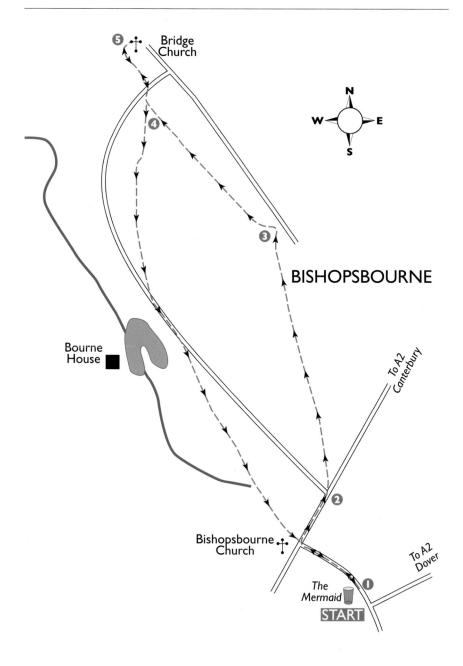

will have sweeping views of Bourne Park House across the ornamental ponds. At the end of the path go through the gate into the wood, but a few feet from the road, turn sharp left along the woodland path heading back out towards the fields.

3 Initially keep to the right-hand tree line, don't take the path striking out into the field. Go through the gate by the trees and follow the path across the field as it drops down into the valley.

4 At the T-junction of paths at the end, turn right and follow the path across the road and into the churchyard. This is St Peter's church in Bridge, the next village along the valley. If you take a look inside you will notice that much of the church's 12th-century origins were lost during an intensive Victorian 'restoration'. The window in the west wall of the nave is a surviving medieval feature.

5 Retrace your steps out of the churchyard and this time keep going straight ahead at point 4. Continue through the gate where the path enters the wood and then drops down onto the road. At the road bear left. After you have passed the entrance to Bourne Park House on your right, take the footpath on your right. You now keep going ahead for about half a mile, crossing the bridge over the river in the middle of the field. The path leaves the field to the left-hand side of the church. Go through the churchyard and you will be at point 2. Now retrace your steps down the lane for a short distance to the pub.

Place of Interest on the Walk

You will be walking through the Bourne Park Estate. The Grade I listed house is a stately Queen Anne period house in rich red brick and stone. Building started in 1704 and the house was said to have been visited by the composer Mozart in 1765 when there was horse riding to be had on the local downs. In the 19th century the owner managed to delay the building of the railway through Bishopsbourne by insisting that it went through a tunnel so as not to spoil the view from his windows. In the early years of the 20th century the grounds of the house saw Kent county cricket games and even test match fixtures. It remains in private hands and there is no admittance to the grounds closer to the house.

The White Cliffs and Folkestone Warren

Walk 19

CAPEL-LE-FERNE

Distance: 4 miles (6.4 km)

Map: OS Explorer 138 Dover, Folkestone & Hythe GR: TR534285

Dog notes: Use the alternative route between points 1 and 3 if you have a dog with you.

How to get there: From the A20 between Folkestone and Dover follow the signs for Capel-le-Ferne. On approaching the village along the B2011 take the left hand turn onto the Old Dover Road. The Lighthouse Inn is on the right hand side.

Parking: At or outside the Lighthouse Inn pub. Postcode: CT18 7HT.

Capel-le-Ferne is a small village which sits right on top of the white cliffs midway between Folkestone and Dover. There are magnificent views along the coastline and on a clear day you can see right across the English Channel to the French coast.

This walk takes you along both the top and along the bottom of the cliffs. There is a new perspective when they tower above you!

From the top we take you down to sea level using one of the lesser-used paths. In places the path has badly deteriorated, which makes it quite a challange, but it is well worth the reward. We have included an alternative route if you prefer.

THE PUB THE LIGHTHOUSE INN is a hotel but features a very large and welcoming bar area, open to all. There are a variety of comfortable indoor seating areas as well as an outside deck, and some picnic tables placed on the cliff top. There is a regular "Pub Classics" menu. Ales on tap were Westerham Spirit of Kent and Sharpe's Doom Bar. ⊕ www.the-lighthouse-inn.co.uk. ☎ 01303 254080.

The Walk

① From outside the pub cross the road and turn left along the cliff-top path. Follow this until you have a static caravan park on your left.

② A few yards ahead a path drops steeply to your right. This is the little-used 'back door' route down into Folkestone Warren – as can be seen by the skeletal remains of the weather-beaten bench and wooden signpost! The path drops steeply down a long succession of wooden steps with the cliffs dramatically rising on one side as you near the sea on the other. In September the bushes are heaving with unharvested blackberries on this 'secret' path. Keep following the path, (in places it will be quite cramped between the railway fence and hedgerows) until you come to the footbridge across the railway on your left. Please note, given the steepness of the descent and the nature of the route you will need to be agile to use this path. As an alternative turn right outside the pub and follow the path to the cliff-top café. Take the path that drops down into Folkestone Warren next to the café. It is still a steep descent but it is made easier by zigzags. Don't take the right-hand turn at the bottom but follow the path out to the footbridge at point 3.

③ Cross over the railway and take the path which keeps the railway closest to your right-hand side. After a few yards, follow the path down the steps towards the sea. At the bottom of the steps take the track the last few yards down to the sea and on to the concrete 'apron'.

④ Retrace your steps back along the broad track but now keep straight ahead, don't go back up the steps. After a while the railway line will be back on your right-hand side again. Keep going over the crest of the hill and back down the other side. Pass through the gate and keep going along what now becomes a minor access road. Continue along the road where it climbs out of the warren up to the Martello Tower which will be on your left.

5 At the tower, turn sharp right along the footpath which runs next to the fence on the right-hand side of the road. Martello Towers are small forts that were built to guard against French invasion in the early years of the 19th century. They take their name from a tower at Mortella Point in Corsica. There were 74 towers along the coastline between here and Seaford in Sussex, of which 25 survive today. This is tower number one. Continue along the path next to the fence, keeping the fence on your left as you climb steeply uphill. At times the summer vegetation will encroach densely on both sides. At the top (where a metal fence is visible on the skyline) turn right. Don't worry if you miss the turn, if you go the wrong way the path will bring you out onto a main road a few yards further on – just retrace your steps. Having made the right-hand turn there is an immediate very short uphill climb back up to the cliff top. Turn left along the cliff-top path (there is a waymarker for the North Downs Way). Now keep along the cliff path following

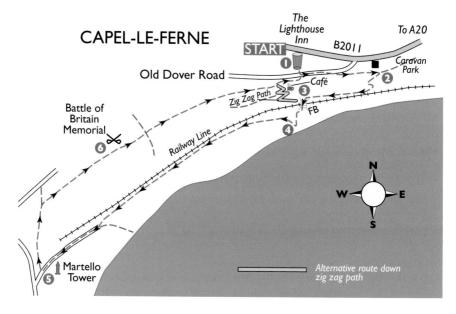

the North Downs Way, do not follow the path which drops back down into the warren. Enjoy the fine views of the English Channel and the White Cliffs of Dover as they march into the distance.

6 After a while the path will emerge onto a well maintained grassy area of land. This is the Battle of Britain Memorial – take some time to explore. The memorial was inspired by a veteran of the battle. As well as the central sculpture of an airman there is a commemorative wall and replicas of Spitfire and Hurricane aircraft. From the air the ground plan of the site appears as a giant aircraft propeller. The memorial invites visitors to pause and remember the bravery and sacrifice of the aircrew who defended this country in the Battle of Britain more than 70 years ago. Continue with the walk along the cliffs. Shortly you will find yourself emerging onto a driveway. Turn left and sharp right after a few yards, be careful not to miss the sign, this is still the coast path. You now just follow the path back to the Lighthouse Inn.

Place of Interest on the Walk

The whole of this route is dominated by the **White Cliffs of Dover**, an iconic symbol of Britain. They are world famous and for centuries have been the gateway to and from the continent, holding a special place in the hearts and minds of many people. Underneath the cliffs Folkestone Warren retains its own unique mix of land and seascapes and its woods have their own eco system. Although Victorian engineers pushed the main Dover – Folkestone railway line through it, it has limited road access and retains a rugged tranquility well worth savoring.

Walmer Castle

Walk 20
DEAL

Distance: 4½ miles (7.2 km)

Map: OS Explorer 150 Canterbury and Isle of Thanet GR: TR377527

How to get there: Head for Deal town centre and then the seafront. Turn left at the seafront. King Street is the first left hand turn off Beach Street after you pass the pier. The pub is a few doors down from the seafront on the left hand side.

Parking: On street parking outside the pub is limited to 2 hours. There are more parking spaces further up the seafront on the right hand side beyond King Street. Postcode: CT14 6HX

Deal, at the far east of the county, came first in the *Daily Telegraph*'s '10 top spots to lay your beach towel', the town also being praised for being 'the genuine Georgian article, with blustery promenade and winding streets.' Despite having no harbour, Deal has a long seafaring history with plenty of places of interest to investigate.

This walk takes you out of the town, along the seafront to the neighbouring town of Walmer and on to the quiet village of Kingsdown. It's essentially a seaside walk taking in several iconic buildings along the way but you also get the chance to walk through the meadows of Hawkshill Freedown where you will get a contrasting change of scenery.

THE PUB As this is the last pub in the book we are introducing you to the latest incarnation of the traditional British pub – the Micropub. Kent saw the UK's first micropub in 2005, the concept is defined as "a small freehouse which listens to its customers, mainly serves cask ales, promotes conversation and shuns all forms of electronic entertainment". The JUST REPROACH is a typical example. It's tiny, taking up the space of a small traditional corner shop –which is what it once was. There are seats and benches around the outside of the room but there is no bar. Attentive waitress service brings the drinks from the cellar to your table. There is no lager, no spirits, no fruit machines, no TV, no music and no mobile phones (apart from the ones nailed to the wall – you get the idea!). What you do get is a unique atmosphere & the lost art of quiet conversation. The pub takes its name from a poem written by Daniel Defoe called 'The Storm' (1703) in which Defoe makes some unflattering remarks about the town. Owned by a father and daughter partnership, the pub has gone from strength to strength since it opened in 2011. Given the micropub concept there is no menu other than local pork pies and local Ashmore cheeses (if you are looking for something more substantial the Sea View Restaurant is a few doors away). Ales on tap on our last visit were Hopdeamon Over the top, Goachers Light and Springhead Surrender. Usually closed Mondays. Remember; when you arrive, don't look for the bar – just sit down!

The Walk

1 From the pub, turn sharp right along King Street. Turn right at the seafront. Initially there will be a section where you have to walk next to the road, but soon the road bears away from the sea and you have a 1½ mile seaside walk all the way to Walmer. There is plenty to see on the way. The pier will be on your left. Take a diversionary stroll to the end and back. It's a recent structure dating only from 1957 and is the third pier on the same site. It's now the only pleasure pier left in Kent. Continuing along the seafront, the Time Ball Tower will be on your right. It was built in 1855; the ball was designed to drop at 1300 GMT to give an accurate time check to offshore shipping. Later on your right is the formidable Deal Castle – an artillery fort constructed by Henry VIII between 1539 and 1540. It formed part of the chain of defensive measures to protect against invasion from France.

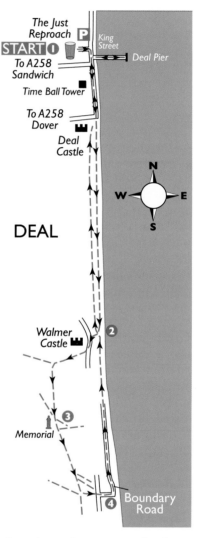

2 After 1½ miles you will see Walmer Castle behind the trees on your right. Leave the coast path and cross a small car park. If you reach a point where you can see the cannon outside the castle, you have gone a little too far and will need to retrace your steps a few yards. Cross the car park and, at the road, turn left in front of the castle. Turn right at the footpath at the end of the castle boundary and follow it uphill until it emerges into a field. This is Hawkshill Freedown. Then turn left and follow the left-hand tree and bush line to the far corner. There is a memorial here to the years when the down was used as a World War I airfield. It has had a variety of other military uses – from being a troop training ground for the castle in the 16th century to being the location of a secret radar base in World War II.

3 At the far corner of the field take the footpath ahead in the same direction, closest to the memorial. Continue in a straight line with high hedges on both sides until you emerge onto a field overlooking the village of Kingsdown with spectacular views over the English

Channel. At the far end of the field follow the waymarker into the trees. There will be a fence on your left-hand side. At a crossroads by a lamp post, turn sharp left and, with the fence still on your left, take the path as it drops down the hillside. At the end, cross over into Boundary Road and walk the few yards up to the seafront.

4 Turn left at the end and take the gravelled road with the beach on your right. Cast your eye over the fascinating variety of designs and ages of the seaside houses, mansions and bungalows which line the road as you walk. After a mile you will be back at point 2. You now return to Deal but with a choice of path, beach or at times broad swathes of grassy park area to walk along – you don't need to retrace your actual steps.

Place of Interest on the Walk

Walmer Castle has the same pedigree as that at Deal – although it was a slightly smaller twin. However Walmer's history took a different course. In the 18th century it became the official residence of the Lord Warden of the Cinque Ports and was gradually modified from a military fortification into a private residence. Various Prime Ministers and prominent politicians were appointed as Lord Warden such as the Duke of Wellington and latterly the late Queen Mother. Parts of the Tudor castle were adapted as living spaces and extensive gardens were established around the property. The castle and gardens are now managed by Historic England and are open daily to visitors. It's well worth a visit – you can even see the original pair of Wellington Boots!

OTHER TITLES FROM COUNTRYSIDE BOOKS

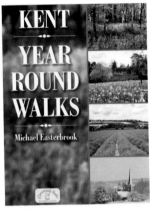

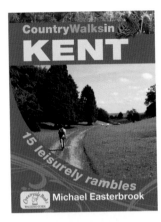

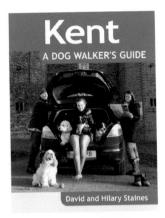

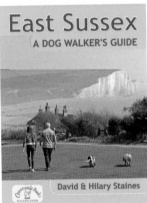

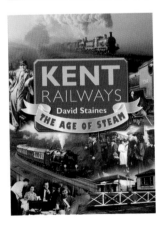

To see the full range of books by Countryside Books then visit
www.countrysidebooks.co.uk

Follow us on